Clinical Nurse Leader:
Transforming Practice, Transforming Care
A model for the clinician at the point of care

Heather M. Monaghan
Diana L. Swihart

VHC VISIONING HEALTHCARE

6731 Professional Parkway W, Suite 105
Sarasota, FL 34240

info@visioninghealthcare.com
or call: 1-877-823-4310 or 941-907-3268
www.visioninghealthcare.com

To my late father who continues to be a great influence in my life, to my wonderful mother who copes with all that life throws at her so well, and to my husband Noel whose ongoing support and belief in me is unwavering.

Heather M. Monaghan

To my beloved husband Stan, to my son Matthew, the other writer in the family, and to my lovely daughter-in-law Gianna, an extraordinary nurse.

Diana L. Swihart

Table of Contents

Acknowledgement .... *xi*
Meet the Authors .... *xiii*
Preface .... *xv*

Chapter 1
Introducing the Clinical Nurse Leader 1

Chapter 2
A Model for the Clinician at the Point of Care 11

Chapter 3
Leadership & Change 21

Chapter 4
Interdisciplinary Relationships 39

Chapter 5
Knowledge Transfer 51

Chapter 6
Outcomes Management 67

Chapter 7
Clinician at the Point of Care 83

Chapter 8
Professional Development 99

Chapter 9
Successes, Challenges, &
Opportunities for the CNL 115

Appendices
Appendix 1: CNL Standards of Conduct 125

Appendix 2: Clinical Nurse Leader Association 129

Appendix 3: Q & A from the Field 131

References **137**

Glossary **141**

Acknowledgement

This book comes from a unique partnership and would not have been possible without the creativity and contributions of Sarah Thomas, an extraordinary editorial assistant and marketing manager, whose patience and confidence in both of us as writers to deliver this manuscript never failed.

Meet the Authors

Meet the Author: Heather M. Monaghan, MHSc, RN

Heather Monaghan has been a Registered Nurse for over 20 years. After a period of working as a Charge Nurse and a Nurse Manager she quickly realized that her passion was in the clinical arena working with her colleagues to make a difference in the way that care was delivered. Over the years her clinical roles have encompassed all of the elements of the Clinical Nurse Leader role and she was fortunate to have become one of the first Nurse Consultants in the United Kingdom, a role not totally dissimilar to the CNL, and which was implemented in order to improve patient outcomes, provide a link between education and practice, and open up career path for nurses who wanted to remain clinically focused. She is a member of the Editorial Board for the *Journal for Nurses in Staff Development* and is the author of the chapter on Change and Change Agents for their Core Curriculum for Staff Development. She has received a variety of awards for her clinical initiatives, published on the implementation of evidence to practice, and is a regular speaker at conferences on the subjects of Nursing Leadership as well as the role of the Clinical Nurse Leader.

Meet the Author: Diana L. Swihart, PhD, DMin, MSN, CS, RN-BC

Dr. Diana Swihart has a widely diverse background in many professional nursing arenas. She is a member of the Editorial Advisory Board for *The Journal of Nursing Regulation*, a member of the Forum for Shared Governance advisory board, and has published and spoken on a number of topics related to nursing, shared governance, preceptorships, competency assessment, spiritual care, ethics, education and staff development, orientation, evidence-based nursing practice and nursing research, and leadership, both nationally and internationally. She has served multiple terms both as an American Nurses Credentialing Center (ANCC) Magnet® Appraiser and as Treasurer for the National Nursing Staff Development Organization (NNSDO). She is currently an ANCC Accreditation Commissioner.

Preface

In an era of constantly evolving technology, healthcare reform, and quality and safety initiatives, a call for practice and care transformation is timely and requisite in order to meet the myriad of healthcare needs. Care delivery is changing exponentially. Time is of the essence as managers and clinicians create a culture of innovation, creativity, productivity, and greatness. Breakthroughs in science and knowledge make it possible to transform care and personalize individual health plans. The Clinical Nurse Leader (CNL) is a key role that will, and is, contributing to transforming care delivery at the point of care while complementing other nursing and professional roles.

The model *Transforming Practice, Transforming Care™* presented in this book is an excellent framework that is uniquely developed and valuable to both organizations and CNLs. Specifically, for organizations, the model provides a venue for building the business case and tools designed to evaluate CNL performance. For the CNL, the model offers marketing and education information when informing others about the value of the role and alignment within healthcare teams. The interwoven elements and threads of leadership and change, interdisciplinary relationships, knowledge transfer, outcomes management, practice at the point of care, and professional development further provide an operational landscape whereby the CNL can be an effective clinician with many opportunities for lifelong learning and professional development.

While the purpose of the CNL is clearly articulated by the American Association of Colleges of Nursing, the methods of integrating the role into existing teams of nurses and other professional groups is not. Likewise, the value and processes for building and sustaining practice and education partnerships remain a challenge. This book is a valuable resource for executive nurse leaders, CNLs, and educators in translating the vision of the role, clarifying and answering questions related to how best to utilize the role, practice application, return on investment, and techniques for sustaining the role.

James L. Harris, DSN, RN-BC, MBA, CNL, FAAN

Chapter 1:
Introducing the Clinical Nurse Leader

Clinical Nurse Leader:
Transforming Practice, Transforming Care

The purpose of this book is to assist executive nurse leaders, educators, and nurses who have completed, or are undertaking, a Clinical Nurse Leader master's degree to translate the theory and vision of the role into one of clearer definition and purpose in the clinical arena. The authors offer this book in response to some of the many questions that have arisen as to how best implement the Clinical Nurse Leader role while respecting the diverse contributions of the rest of the healthcare team.

The origins of the Clinical Nurse Leader date back to 1999 when the Institute of Medicine (IOM) published *To Err is Human: Building a Safer Health System.* This ground-breaking report identified that between 44,000 and 98,000 Americans died each year as the result of medical errors and moved the nation to action. With the nursing shortage deepening at that time and an increasingly-fragmented health care system providing fertile ground for preventable mistakes, the American Association of Colleges of Nursing (AACN) looked at how nursing could play its part in improving patient outcomes by strengthening nursing leadership at the point at which care is delivered. The subsequent discussions led to the publication of the *White Paper on the Role of the Clinical Nurse Leader*[SM] (AACN, 2007) and the creation of the first new nursing role in the USA in more than thirty-five years.

The *Clinical Nurse Leader*, who may be defined as

an advanced generalist, responsible for the provision of quality, safe, effective care for his or her defined patient/client population, is a registered nurse who

- is educated to graduate level with a master's degree or higher;
- works with intra and interdisciplinary team members;
- applies evidence-based practice (EBP);
- minimizes risk and maximizes the quality of clinical care delivered;
- contributes to the assessment of a cohort of assigned patients with complex healthcare needs;
- has an entrepreneurial spirit;
- is equipped to meet the rigors and demands of the ever-changing healthcare agenda in a particular clinical environment.

In short,

the Clinical Nurse Leader is responsible for improving clinical outcomes through leadership at the point of care delivery.

There are many graduate programs available in the USA for the aspiring Clinical Nurse Leader (CNL), all of which provide a strong theoretical and clinical foundation to meet the complexities healthcare demands of the nursing profession and the role. However, a dissonance still remains between what is taught and how the CNL role is applied to practice, with many questions remaining about it including the most fundamental and overarching question:

"Why do I even need a Clinical Nurse Leader when I already have a Clinical Nurse Specialist (CNS), a Clinical Nurse Educator (CNE), and an Advanced Registered Nurse Practitioner (ARNP)?"

It is true that some of the early Clinical Nurse Leaders have been recruited from these very groups. Due to a shortage of funding, this recruitment method has been the only way many facilities have been able to introduce this new role, which has further complicated understanding of its uniqueness. The authors believe Clinical Nurse Leaders are an integral part of the clinical team and have a clearly defined role that is complimentary to their master's prepared colleagues. In order to understand this belief, it is important to look closer at the functions of Clinical Nurse Leaders.

Many health professionals are confused about what the role of the Clinical Nurse Leader is and what it is not.

Whenever the question arises as to the difference between the CNS, the CNE, and the ARNP, it is important to consider two questions:

1. Is the role based *at the point of care?*
2. Is the role regarded as a *generalist* or a *specialist?*

The CNL is not a Clinical Nurse Specialist (CNS).

The CNS functions within the macrosystem (organizational or system-wide) and is not usually based in one particular unit. He or she is generally educated to graduate level and focuses on one specific patient population, such as cardiovascular, diabetic, psychiatric, pediatric, or geriatric. The CNS accepts referrals to review practice or a particular aspect of a patient's care plan from anywhere in the facility and is involved in the implementation of EBP through policy development for his or her particular group. By the very nature of the title, he or she is a *specialist* in one particular patient population.

In contrast, the Clinical Nurse Leader works at the microsystem (unit/floor level), is based in one unit or physical area, and is regarded as an advanced *generalist*. He or she may have a variety of different types of patients within the assigned unit or area, such as those found in a Medical/Surgical unit. While CNLs share the commonality of providing quality EBP with the CNS, Clinical Nurse Leaders spend much of their time working with staff directly or within their defined point of care to implement evidence-based policies and guidelines in order to effect change and improve patient outcomes.

The CNL may call on the CNS to provide a consultation when an area of concern arises requiring the knowledge or skill of a specialist for a particular patient population, for example, when a patient does not respond to nursing care or other therapeutic interventions as expected (AACN, 2007).

The CNL is not a Clinical Nurse Educator (CNE).

While there are additional educational components to both these roles, CNEs work predominantly at the macrosystem level, even though they may be positioned within a specified clinical unit or area. They are responsible for the assessment, planning, implementation, and evaluation of clinical and non-clinical programs and learning activities. While not regarded as having the same specialist knowledge as a CNS, CNEs are generally experienced in the clinical areas in which they work and may be responsible for preparing staff nurses for national certifications in specialties or subspecialties of nursing practice, as well as providing orientation, coaching, in-services, and education programs targeted at the competencies and learning needs of their assigned units or areas. CNEs are responsible for participating in the strategic educational planning and delivery of national, state, and organizational mandated updates and for facilitating appropriate educational programs to meet the ongoing re-licensure and accreditation requirements of clinical staff.

While they may work in classrooms and/or clinical settings, CNEs are not generally regarded as point of care practitioners. For this reason, along with the styles of education they deliver (*i.e.*, simulations, case study analyses, and competency assessments), they have a clear differentiation in their responsibilities and functions from those of Clinical Nurse Leaders. However, the two groups do work closely together in their identified roles. CNLs may determine aspects of unit practice they believe cannot be effectively addressed through individual employee development in one clinical area alone. They may then ask the CNE to liaise with colleagues at the macrosystem level to ascertain if this is an identified or potential need in other units within the organization or system, who will then establish the appropriate education.

The CNL is not an Advanced Registered Nurse Practitioner (ARNP).

The ARNP and the Clinical Nurse Leader have both completed education at the master's level, and in the case of the former, maybe even a Doctor in Nursing Practice (DNP) program. The ARNP is further trained in the process of diagnosing and treating minor, and in some cases more complex, medical conditions. ARNPs also focus on one specialty, such as cardiovascular, geriatrics, pediatrics, or primary care and work closely with a physician or physician group. They are often at the first point of entry to healthcare and work within the medical model of diagnosing, history-taking, conducting physical examinations, and ordering tests delineated within their scopes of practice.

While the Clinical Nurse Leader graduate program prepares CNLs with the skills to be able to complete physical assessments of patients to a level beyond that of a regular nurse, it does not meet the criteria for Advanced Practice Nursing (APN). For example, ARNPs practice autonomously and independently under their licensure, education, and professional credentials. While CNLs are empowered within their designated authority, facility policies and protocols, and their intra and interdisciplinary relationships to act as a coordinator of care, they do not function as an independent practitioner.

***

The CNS, CNE, and ARNP are not the only roles confusing the implementation of the Clinical Nurse Leader. There is also a need to look at two other members of the unit team the CNL will develop close and supportive relationships with and for whom some people feel roles may overlap: the Charge Nurse and the Nurse Manager.

While the differences between the CNL, CNS, CNE, and ARNP can be clearly identified, by whether the roles are generalist, specialist, primarily *at the point of care,* or at an organizational level, the distinctions between the CNL, Charge Nurse, and Nurse Manager are best determined by simply asking:

Does this role have a human resource or budgetary management component?

These are the two key elements that most clinical staff identify as part of the role of a manager, rather than a leader.

The CNL is not a Charge Nurse.

Charge Nurses work closely with Nurse Managers and have a large management component to their role. They ensure the seamless flow of unit activities throughout the shift, allocating admissions to appropriate staff, ensuring discharges go smoothly, checking orders, managing any scheduling changes required through call-ins, and handling crises (*i.e.*, patients' complaints) along with any other challenges that present during their shift. While there is a trend towards eliminating caseloads for Charge Nurses, many are still required to care for the same number of patients as their colleagues, while managing the unit at the same time.

Clinical Nurse Leaders, however, are responsible for supporting safe clinical care at the point in which it is delivered and carry no responsibility for the day-to-day running of the shift, unit, or area they work within. Their caseload is comprised of all the patients within their assigned unit or clinical area rather than an allocation of a specific patient or patients. For example, if they work on a unit with thirty patients, they are responsible for the quality of clinical care delivered to all thirty patients, not just the individual nursing care of five or six.

The CNL is not a Nurse Manager.

It is clear that the distinction between the Clinical Nurse Leader and the Nurse Manager is even more evident when considering that the latter is a manager to all the staff on the unit, often including the Clinical Nurse Leader. The Nurse Manager is responsible and accountable for scheduling, recruitment, counseling and disciplinary actions, negotiating union issues, dealing with serious complaints and service recovery, meeting budgetary constraints, and has the positional authority to act on his or her decisions.

The Nurse Manager does share one significant goal with the Clinical Nurse Leader. They are both responsible for ensuring the best quality care is provided to their patients. The Nurse Manager facilitates this through many of the previously identified aspects of his or her non-clinical role. The Clinical Nurse Leader will achieve similar outcomes through intra and interdisciplinary teamwork at the point of care delivery, managing risk through educating staff, implementing evidence-based practice, evaluating practice-based evidence (PBE), and providing leadership and expertise in safe, quality care for his or her assigned patient cohort.

While both may be described as leaders, they have very different approaches in implementing their leadership roles. *Horizontal leadership* is an integral part of being a Clinical Nurse Leader and enables the CNL to function within and across the interprofessional boundaries. Nurse Managers are generally more traditional and lead through *vertical management*, using the hierarchical structures of an organization to oversee and guide the tasks and staff activities of the unit to achieve their goals.

Clearly, the Clinical Nurse Leader is a unique and critical missing link in the chain of professional healthcare clinicians with the goal of providing high quality, safe clinical care from the macro to the microsystem level.

The model *Transforming Practice, Transforming Care™* presented in the remaining chapters of this book describes the essential elements for successful implementation of this exciting, new professional nurse role, as well as identifying how it aligns with the concepts of excellence at the point of care delivery described in the

Clinical Nurse Leader:
Transforming Practice, Transforming Care

American Nurses Credentialing Center's (ANCC) Magnet Recognition Program® (2008).

Chapter 2:
A Model for the Clinician at the Point of Care

While the *purpose* of the Clinical Nurse Leader (CNL) in *ensuring high quality, safe, outcomes-based care* is clear, the *process* of integrating the role into existing teams of nurses and other professional groups is not. Nurses have only to reflect back to the introduction of the Advanced Registered Nurse Practitioner (ARNP) some years ago to recognize there may be challenges with implementing the CNL role, including the predictable resistance to change that is often seen due to a lack of understanding something new.

The *Transforming Practice, Transforming Care™* model for the clinician at the point of care clarifies the role of the Clinical Nurse Leader and is an invaluable tool to any organization in

- marketing the role to senior executives in order to obtain funding for a CNL;
- creating a job description that encompasses all the essential requirements of a CNL, by which the organization can establish criteria to include the role into its existing career ladders;
- developing a framework to evaluate the performance of the individual CNL and the improvement in outcomes achieved.

Additionally, the model provides Clinical Nurse Leaders with

- clarity of their role;

- a tool to educate nursing and interdisciplinary colleagues, as well as patients and patient families on the CNL's role, responsibilities, and how the CNL works within the healthcare team;
- a means of identifying strengths and weaknesses in the skills required to be effective in their role, and a guideline for assessing professional learning and development needs.

The model for Transforming Practice, Transforming Care™ consists of six elements:

Leadership and Change
Interdisciplinary Relationships
Knowledge Transfer
Outcomes Management
Clinician at the Point of Care
Professional Development

The first four elements represent the areas of skill, knowledge, and behavior required of the Clinical Nurse Leader in order to be an effective clinician in the fifth element *at the point of care*. The sixth element is a thread interwoven between the previous five and represents the *professional development* of the individual CNL and those with whom he or she works.

Leadership and Change

As an individual who is required to "assume guardianship of the nursing profession" (AACN, 2007, p 3) through academic and clinical preparation, the Clinical Nurse Leader is required to translate responsibility to practice through a professionalism that not only represents the scope and standards of a master's prepared Registered Nurse with a CNL® certification but which also portrays a feeling of safety, trust, and integrity from the colleagues, patients, and families they serve. CNLs need to understand the concepts of horizontal rather than vertical leadership, the skills for becoming a transformational leader, and the ability to work with colleagues from a variety of disciplines, while remaining steadfast in their ability to lead teams and change. They advocate for patients and families through the provision of evidence-based practice aimed at ensuring a safe journey throughout the healthcare continuum. Being comfortable in the roles of leader and change agent is crucial in building and nurturing effective

Interdisciplinary Relationships.

As a centralized coordinator of care, the need for strong, accurate communication skills and an understanding and respect for the many different professionals they work with is essential. *To walk in someone else's shoes for the day* is an excellent way to obtain this understanding and an ideal opportunity to educate others on the CNL role. The skills embedded in horizontal leadership and the concepts of being a servant leader underpin all four components of the model. However, they are particularly appropriate in this element when the more traditional styles of vertical leadership seen in healthcare organizations would be inappropriate and potentially destructive to the team dynamics and the ability of the CNL to function effectively. Excellent communication skills and an ability to actively listen to others are key attributes when looking at this and the third element of the model,

Knowledge Transfer.

The Clinical Nurse Leader provides education to direct caregivers at the point of care delivery, members of the interdisciplinary team, patients, and relatives. This may be delivered in a variety of ways, and an understanding of the principles of adult education, effective coaching and feedback, and patient learning strategies are all essential in order to be able to transfer knowledge in a way that makes a difference, is understood, and is appropriate. CNLs must be well-grounded in working with practice-based evidence, quality monitors, and

15

healthcare informatics. They pull many resources and research into evidence-based practice when contributing to standards of care, protocols, and procedures that support best practices and

Outcomes Management.

Returning to the origins of the Clinical Nurse Leader, it is in this area the role will be measured for its level of success and value to the patient and the organization. The CNL requires a variety of skills to achieve this element, including a functional knowledge of risk management and prevention, core measures, data analysis and evaluation, systems analysis, critical reasoning, and an ability to synthesize data from a variety of sources in order to identify process improvements for nursing and other members of the interdisciplinary team. Outcomes management exposes the CNL to a number of other groups and diverse committees. It is important CNLs remain clear about their role and do not get drawn into meetings that might take them away from their primary purpose or affect their ability to make a clinical impact as a

Clinician at the Point of Care.

Of the six elements, the Clinician at the Point of Care causes the most confusion. The questions of what constitutes a caseload and how much time should be spent *at the point of care* will be addressed later in this book. Undoubtly, however, the strength of the CNL lies in its proximity to direct caregivers across all clinical settings.

While they are not ARNPs, CNLs are educated at the graduate level with advanced skills in health assessment and the associated knowledge base. They synthesize clinical data to determine the most appropriate intervention for the patient, as well as make sound clinical judgments while planning and/or changing the care plan in partnership with the interdisciplinary team. It is important to remember that the CNL has a responsibility to promote good health as well as caring for those who are unwell. One of their most significant responsibilities is to empower direct caregivers with the skills to provide outcomes-driven care underpinned by evidence while practicing a patient-centric approach. Role modeling, teaching, and empowering others, while continuing to grow personally and professionally, lead into the final element of the model,

Professional Development.

The thread of Professional Development is woven through all of the elements of the model, depicting how CNLs fold their own development into every aspect of their role. Also, they are intricately involved, both formally and informally, in the professional development of others. For CNLs, teaching and mentoring begins when they define their role and potential contributions to the leaders who hire them, when they clarify their responsibilities and duties to their intra and interdisciplinary team members, and when they actively implement their work at the point of care. As advanced generalists, CNLs are constantly monitoring trends in healthcare, scanning the environments of practice, and reviewing the literature for best practices and new evidence to improve patient care outcomes. Professional development is seen as an ever-occurring opportunity for CNLs and those they impact.

***

While the model provides a practical focus to the implementation of the Clinical Nurse Leader role, it is underpinned by a combination of perspectives, including

1. The 10 Assumptions for Preparing Clinical Nurse Leaders identified by the AACN (2007) as suggested requirements for the development of the master's level curriculum in preparation of the CNL role;

2. The Fundamental Aspects of the CNL role as determined by the AACN White Paper on the role of the Clinical Nurse Leader^SM (2007);

3. the five components of the New Model for the ANCC Magnet Recognition Program® (2008) as they relate to nursing and nursing development, identified as follows:

   - Transformational Leadership
   - Structural Empowerment
   - Exemplary Professional Practice
   - New Knowledge, Innovations, and Improvements
   - Empirical Quality Outcomes

4. experiences of past and present Clinical Nurse Leaders;

5. the extensive clinical, leadership, and educational experience of both authors.

Each element of the model, discussed in the next six chapters, provides the reader with a detailed look at how each can be applied to practice, the skills required to achieve competency in each area, and each element's connection to the components of the Magnet® model. Also, the narrative will incorporate a pragmatic look at how some of the challenges can be overcome to make this role a success for the CNL, their colleagues, executive leaders, and, most important, their patients.

Chapter 3:
Leadership & Change

For many Clinical Nurse Leaders, the prospect of being in such a significant leadership role will be daunting, particularly in the early days when it feels like *all eyes will be upon them*. While the graduate programs that underpin their preparation specify an entry standard of having a bachelor's degree in nursing and being licensed as a Registered Nurse through NCLEX examination, there are no consistent requirements to have practiced for a pre-determined number of years or to have been exposed to a role that provided training or experience at some level of leadership.

The leadership skills required of the CNL are both challenging and diverse. The relatively black-and-white approaches needed to manage a group of patients or to carry out routine tasks and procedures make way for the broader demands of horizontal leadership, facilitating change, and the provision of lateral integration of care required in the delivery of quality care outcomes. As they make the paradigm shift into the world of gray, CNLs engage in new depths and approaches to collaboration, communication, and relationship building as they work with their intra and interdisciplinary colleagues on a level they may not have experienced before.

Making the successful transition from direct caregiver to leader at the point of care is crucial to the credibility of the role.

It is important, therefore, that the Nurse Manager and executive level nurse recognize this and ensure that support networks are put in place. This includes a personal mentor in order for CNLs to develop their skills in an environment that does not expect too much of them too soon and is willing to allow the role to evolve.

While it is well established that the Clinical Nurse Leader

provides clinical leadership to the nursing and interdisciplinary team to effectively manage transformational change and facilitate an empowered workforce,

there is still some confusion about what this actually looks like. What is certain is that the successful Clinical Nurse Leaders require

- an understanding of horizontal and other styles of leadership and their application to practice;
- an awareness of how their microsystem fits into the wider goals of the organization;
- excellent communication skills that facilitate learning and encourage safe practice;
- an entrepreneurial spirit that enables them to think organizationally as well as clinically;
- an understanding of their role and influence in healthcare reform;
- an understanding of change theory and how to address resistance.

***

The association of horizontal leadership within the role of the Clinical Nurse Leader is a defining one and is a style that has so rarely been articulated as belonging to a particular nurse role.

The term *horizontal leadership* is used to identify an approach where the leader's **influence** comes not from the power and authority of their position (as seen in the more traditional vertical hierarchies of healthcare) but one which is earned through knowledge, education, and respect. To facilitate this, CNLs require an understanding of how the approaches of transformational and relational leadership underpin the horizontal approach they will use in practice.

The difference between horizontal and the more traditional, vertical style of leadership

is best demonstrated by examining the core concepts of the roles of the CNL and the Unit/Nurse Manager. The latter is recognized as both a leader and a manager, who is responsible for the management of human resources and the fiscal budget and who has, by their position in the hierarchy, been designated with a level of authority to perform that role. They also handle disciplinary issues and complaints, represent the unit at meetings at the organizational level, and act as the link between the executive level leaders and the staff in their unit in translating into practice the organization's mission, vision, and values. (Figure 3.1)

Conversely, Clinical Nurse Leaders have no human resource or unit fiscal management responsibilities. While not having any formal positional authority over the direct caregivers working with their patient population, they have, however, been empowered to change plans of care when required, delegate and supervise the care given, and deliver and manage improvements in patient safety and clinical outcomes in line with the organization's goals.

Figure 3.1: Traditional Vertical Hierarchy

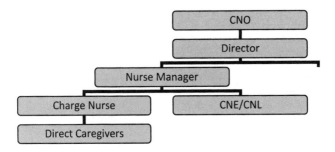

It is a particularly important point to get across to all staff within an organization that the CNL role is not "yet another layer of management" but rather a tier in the career ladder for the professional direct caregiver.

The process of *horizontal leadership* occurs where the care is delivered in a microsystem, a unit structure wherein the Clinical Nurse Leader analyzes, manages, improves outcomes, and provides an opportunity for implementing innovative patient care within an assigned patient population. This lateral integration is generally comprised of

- relationships among patients and healthcare professionals;
- direct care processes (for assessing, diagnosing, treating, evaluating, and managing plans of care);
- measurements of quality and safety;
- patients' functional status;
- risk;

- patient satisfaction;
- cost effectiveness of outcomes-based practice.

As their leadership role *fans out* to engage everyone involved with their patient cohort (Figure 3.2), they bring to the process the skills and strengths of relational leadership.

Figure 3.2: Horizontal Leadership through the Lateral Integration of Care

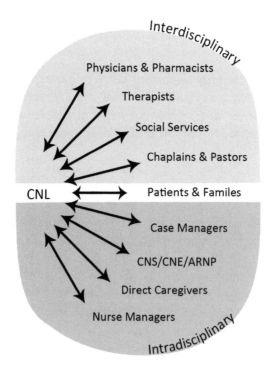

For example at the beginning of a shift, the CNL might listen to report on all of the patients on their assigned unit or area. During the report, they may note changes to be considered related to design, implementation, and/or evaluation of plans of care. Then, they will meet with the appropriate team members to determine how best to coordinate the care and effect changes in the care plans based on patient concerns, laboratory results, reports, and care rounds. Also, they would factor into their work any education or coaching to be given to staff, patients, families, and/or interdisciplinary team members related to evidence-based patient care outcomes and quality indicators.

This networking approach has many benefits, including recognizing that everyone has a part to play in the decision-making process. With the lack of a vertical hierarchy, the CNL and the healthcare team are able to respond to the needs of the patient in a timelier manner.

***

Transformational leaders influence others to do what they want them to do, rather than dictate, demand, or micromanage. They show their colleagues the direction and facilitate them getting there.

As *transformational leaders,* it is the role of the CNL to track and create valuable and positive changes in those with whom they work, helping them develop into leaders and more confident practitioners. Their **power** comes from using the tools of influence, knowledge, and role modeling. They assist colleagues in understanding how their role in the delivery of quality care translates to meeting the organization's goals. As inspirational leaders, they challenge peers to take greater ownership for their own work. In order to feel confident enough to do this, however, they need to understand the strengths and weaknesses of others and align them with tasks that optimize their performance at the point of care delivery.

The Clinical Nurse Leader guides the lateral integration of care through a process of horizontal leadership at the point of care while keeping in mind the wider goals of the organization.

It can often be difficult for CNLs to understand how they can work in a tiered system that supports a vertical hierarchy, which also expects them to lead in a horizontal way. Understanding the purpose of the macro, meso, and microsystems within this structure are essential to establishing effective working patterns.

- A *Healthcare macrosystem* is made up of teams who *determine* the goals of the organization, create the structures that provide the foundation to achieving them, establish the systems by which they will be monitored, and allocate the resources.

- *Departments/Divisions mesosystems* are made up of teams that represent the structures (risk management, shared governance, quality systems, human resources, clinical and environmental services) which *translate* the goals of the organization.

- *Clinical microsystems* are made up of teams that work collaboratively and focus on specific functions and activities to *deliver* the goals of the organization at the point at which care is delivered. (Figure 3.3)

Figure 3.3: A Systems Model of Organizational Structure

WHOLE ORGANIZATION
- Nursing Services
- Senior Leaders
- CEO, COO, CFO
- CMO, CNO, CIO

MAJOR DEPARTMENTS/DIVISIONS/SYSTEMS
- Nursing, Medicine, Informatics, Women's Health, Pediatrics
- Clinical Service Lines
- Strategies & Operations

FRONT-LINE NURSING UNITS (Smaller Functional Units)
- *Clinical Nurse Leaders*
- Patients
- Families
- CNS, CNE, ARNP
- Nurse Managers
- Healthcare Providers- Nurses, Physicians, Pharmacists, Therapists, Social Workers
- Other Team Members
- Processes

Working with an ever widening network of caregivers and systems to overcome the challenges of fragmentation and complexities in today's healthcare environment (that lead to so many of the preventable errors and safety challenges that occur in practice), CNLs need to pull information from the many sources available within the organizational structure in which they work. By developing a network throughout the meso and macro systems, they are able to facilitate the interrelationships and collaborations necessary to achieve their goals at the microsystem level.

One of the biggest challenges for all new CNLs is to reach a level of comfort in working and communicating with all members of the intra and interdisciplinary team in unfamiliar ways, elevating their role as patient advocate to a new level.

Maxfield et al (2005) demonstrates the importance of Crucial Conversations® in the report *Silence Kills-The Seven Crucial Conversations® in Healthcare*: Defined as a "*discussion between two or more people where (1) stakes are high, (2) opinions vary, and (3) emotions run strong*" (Patterson et al, 2002, p 3). These seven crucial conversations focus on

- broken rules;
- mistakes;
- lack of support;
- incompetence;
- poor teamwork;
- disrespect;
- micromanagement;

and were identified as ones in which healthcare workers had the most difficulty holding but, without which, patient outcomes were significantly affected.

For Clinical Nurse Leaders, who may often find themselves in situations where a conversation is crucial, or turns into one as they feel the adrenaline flow and their fight/flight response engage, it is important to learn to do the following:

- *Recognize the power of dialogue and how to use it*, as words can be as damaging as they are healing when used carelessly
- *Stay focused on what is important* and not allow themselves to be taken along another path
- *Anticipate when safety is at risk and make it safe to talk about anything* by taking the conversation to a more private place, thus respecting confidentiality in the process
- *Focus on staying in dialogue when emotions run high* by mentally walking away until emotions are calmer, as people rarely hear or process information accurately when angry or upset
- *Be prepared to admit they may be wrong* in order to maintain and build integrity, respect, and confidence with co-workers
- *Speak persuasively, not abrasively*, while stating the facts and staying on topic without shifting into aggressive, cynical, or whining behaviors
- *Listen carefully when others express their own anger through noise or silence,* as silence can be a powerful tool for manipulating outcomes

and a "louder" influence in a conversation than noise or reason

- *Bring the conversation to a close with a solution or identified plan*

***

Additionally, the CNL must understand the basics of healthcare finance, economics, and fiscal responsibility within the macro, meso, and microsystems when managing their patient cohort, as well as further embracing the principles of entrepreneurship as they try new ways to achieve better outcomes and not be afraid to challenge the status quo.

While it has been identified that Clinical Nurse Leaders do not hold the budget for the unit in which they work, they need to recognize that they do have a fiscal contribution to make related to the finances and economics embedded in the strategic workings of the organization. When coordinating care, they quantify, develop, and leverage environmental, human, and material resources to achieve the best possible patient care outcomes while keeping costs down. They also identify, compare, and evaluate activities and procedures across institutions to determine the most appropriate when considering the effects of healthcare financing on care access and patient outcomes. It is a misconception that change costs money. In fact, with the discontinuation of reimbursement to hospitals from Medicare for preventable conditions, there is a clear case for the implementation of evidence-based practice.

Clinical Nurse Leaders contribute to the shaping and delivery of healthcare policy, which may include a combination of regulations, legislation, public policy, ethics, standards of care, scopes of practice, and politics. As leaders they contribute to the macrosystem level of the organization by delivering the mission, vision, and values that have been translated by the mesosystem they work within.

As a collaborative leader for the unit team, the Clinical Nurse Leader advocates for improvements in healthcare systems/organizations, policies, procedures and the professional roles of other nurses and healthcare providers.

As transformational leaders, they use a process of systems thinking and evidence to solve problems, develop strategies and solutions, and challenge existing practice in order to effect change and lessen healthcare disparities. They collaborate and communicate with diverse teams to improve quality, advance professional practice, and ensure safe, effective, efficient patient care outcomes.

***

In the rapidly-shifting, complex world of healthcare, Clinical Nurse Leaders are required to be able to manage immediate change at the point of care as it occurs.

Their presence on patient care units strengthens the care provided, creating and supporting a more committed and effective workforce (Hartranft et al, 2007). They monitor and evaluate the care, suggest changes to improve outcomes, and communicate with the healthcare team to discuss patient observations, progress, and changes in care plans. Their accessibility to other groups beyond their nursing and unit colleagues allows them to obtain data that both informs and evaluates the clinical outcomes they are empowered to manage and change.

Leading change at the point of care requires very different skills than those required by an individual leading an organizational change. While the latter will use traditional styles of change management such as Lewin's theory of change (1951), the Clinical Nurse Leader, when working with individuals, will use tools such as

- coaching and feedback;
- Crucial Conversations® (Patterson et al, 2002); reflective practice;
- Dreyfus model of skill acquisition–Novice to Expert (Benner, 1984);
- Situational Leadership (Hersey & Blanchard, 1988).

When working with teams, the CNL may employ

- *Appreciative Inquiry* based upon appreciating and valuing the best of what is, envisioning what might be, and dialoging what should be as the change is implemented and evaluated (Cooperrider & Whitney, 2005);

- I_2E_2 *Leading Lasting Change,* an approach based on a healthcare-focused cyclical model that embraces appreciative inquiry and advocates engagement of everyone to help maximize each person's contribution to the collective good through *inspiration* (I_1), strategic, operational, and tactical *infrastructure* (I_2), *education* (E_1), and *evidence* (E_2) (Felgen, 2007).

Acting as a change agent within the micro and meso systems of healthcare, the Clinical Nurse Leader needs to have

- the ability to learn "on the fly";
- adaptability;
- flexibility;
- the ability to engage in "just-in-time" learning and application of new information;
- clear and accurate communication skills;
- self-confidence;
- a healthy sense of humor.

Clinical Nurse Leaders can positively effect change

through an understanding of

- the basic concepts of change that enable them to apply a variety of different change theories to practice;
- problem solving at the point of care;
- engaging in servant leadership and relationship building;
- providing options, time, and encouragement through teaching, coaching, and mentoring along each step/phase of the change process;
- remembering that change *starts with one*: the CNL who is able to see the need to change, moves to affect or facilitate that change, and follows through to the finish in achieving and sustaining the change (Black & Gregersen, 2008).

Whenever a change takes place, whether in the introduction of their role, a change in clinical practice, or even just providing feedback, it is inevitable the CNL will meet some resistance and upset.

Although change can be energizing, creative, and result in new and more effective ways of providing care, like all change agents, CNLs require a clear understanding of the dynamics of change, the reasons for resistance, and the strategies for helping their teams move forward to inform and transform practice.

Resistance arises from fear. Change is often seen as threatening, uncomfortable, unfamiliar, and/or just not worth the trouble, regardless of how necessary it might be. One example of this is the CNL engaging the intra and interdisciplinary team members in implementing telehealth or telemedicine. When advanced technology or information systems for patient care are implemented throughout the organization and staff is required to learn how to use the new system to manage clinical records, it can feel overwhelming. The healthcare team members may resist if *change fatigue* occurs with too many changes occurring at once, in too short a time, or when implementation takes too long to complete.

It is not difficult to lead people where they want to go or help them do what they have always done, but real and lasting change demands more.

CNLs must help their teams—like so many of their patients—to see why change is necessary and what their roles are in achieving that change. One of the best ways they can facilitate and effect positive change is to be mindful of how they might react in similar circumstances. Then, they must guide, challenge, influence, coach, and affirm others through the change with patience, compassion, empowered teamwork, and a commitment to the improvements in care delivery the change will bring. This is horizontal, transformational leadership in action.

Finally, this first element of the *Transforming Practice, Transforming Care™* model is a reminder to all CNLs how their leadership role extends far beyond the units in which they work. As authentic leaders, they not only lead on patient safety and clinical outcomes, but are also leaders within their profession. The CNL *Standards of Conduct* (CNC, 2010) reflects their commitment to role modeling five moral areas embedded in their leadership role:

- altruism
- accountability
- human dignity
- integrity
- social justice

These standards flow through all other elements of this model. (Appendix 1)

POINT TO MAGNET

The Clinical Nurse Leader advanced generalist role is firmly set within the culture of transformational and horizontal leadership, empowerment, professional and interdisciplinary team relationships, and the lateral integration of care services across the clinical microsystem in which the CNL practices.

Transformational leadership in nursing practice is so compelling the American Nurses Credentialing Center (ANCC) identified this as one of five core components in their new Magnet model in 2008. CNLs are recognized as significant change agents in their microsystem while adhering to the goals of the meso and macrosystems, using their spheres of influence and responsibility to contribute to achieving sustainable and lasting improvements in evolving environments of care.

Chapter 4:
Interdisciplinary Relationships

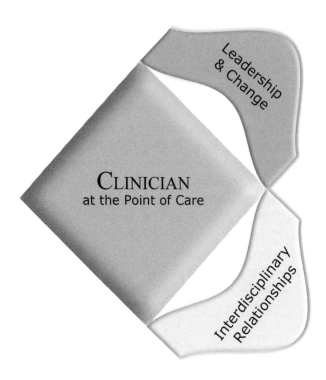

Working with the interdisciplinary team is the perfect opportunity to piece together the horizontal leadership of the Clinical Nurse Leader and the process of laterally integrating the care of the patient in whatever clinical setting they work.

Within the element of *interdisciplinary relationships,* Clinical Nurse Leaders assume accountability for the care outcomes of an assigned patient population within a specific clinical area. Also, they assimilate and apply current research and evidence-based information into designing, implementing, evaluating, and changing their patients' care plans as required through the process of lateral integration. In order to be effective, they need to overcome the functional and professional silos that may present in their day-to-day activities and which are extremely counterproductive to providing efficient, effective, safe patient care.

While the breakdown of these professional silos will ultimately be seen through interprofessional education (IPE) at diploma, bachelor's, master's level and beyond, the functional (departmental) ones need to be addressed by leadership at the most senior level of the organization. The CNL, however, has a unique opportunity through their role as a horizontal leader to bring all the disciplines together within their microsystem in a way that is non-threatening, complimentary, and safe.

This process of building relationships and moving towards patient-focused, rather than discipline-specific, goals is crucial. The term *interdisciplinary,* rather than *multi-disciplinary,* is used throughout this book. This is purposeful. Not only does it define the working relationship the CNL needs to develop with their professional colleagues in order to be successful in their role, but also it serves as an indicator of the way they are expected to function.

Traditionally, multi-disciplinary working has been associated with the combined approach of a variety of different professionals working towards their own discipline-specific goals that did not necessarily reflect a holistic approach to the care of the patient or the family (Jessop, 2007).

As healthcare moves towards a more patient-focused, patient-centric model of care, the attributes of interdisciplinary relationships and teams grounded in collegial relationships are more representative of the CNLs working environment. Communication is enhanced by collaboration as the paradigm shifts towards a more united approach to goal setting and outcomes management with a clearer acceptance of the potential for overlap of professional boundaries when meeting care delivery goals.

For this element of the *Transforming Practice, Transforming Care™* model to be effective, the following must be present

- an in-depth understanding of each healthcare team member's roles;
- open and respectful communication;

- empowerment of every person involved in planning and implementing the care, including the patient and family members.

Clinical Nurse Leaders work in a complex, challenging, and constantly changing environment of care, as a respected member of the intra and interdisciplinary teams. This requires experience and skills in communication, team coordination, relationship-building, conflict management, and advocacy.

As part of the **intradisciplinary team,** which includes other nursing colleagues, such as the Charge Nurse, Nurse Manager, CNS, CNE, ARNP, and the Case Manager, the CNL has responsibilities to

- supervise, delegate, and facilitate nursing procedures and clinical interventions as part of the interdisciplinary care plan for their cohort of patients;
- role model critical thinking skills through effective communication (active listening, speaking, and writing);
- facilitate professional development activities;
- provide oversight, training, and mentoring in the lateral integration of care delivery;
- provide feedback to the unit-based practice council or unit meeting;
- help to translate and implement organizational goals into their unit;
- suggest solutions for unit-based challenges and evaluate interventions;
- initiate new approaches to care.

As an integral part of their **interdisciplinary team**, which includes therapists, physicians, pharmacists, social workers, and others, CNLs also contribute by

- teaching, educating, coaching, and delegating skilled tasks to team members, patients, and family members as appropriate;
- facilitating group participation, interactions, brainstorming, and problem solving;
- providing relationship-based care with care team members;
- engaging the team in evidence-based practice (EBP), research activities, and quality improvement strategies through data collection and application of technology to practice;
- contributing to creation and sustaining of a positive culture of safety through an empowered workforce;
- influencing care and practice decisions by engaging nurses and other interdisciplinary team members through the use of data, information, and outcomes within the context of learning and skills development;
- advocating for the needs of the patient.

For CNLs, the pattern of their collegial relationships and the capacity to form them are more important than tasks, functions, roles, and positions. This pattern enables them to be effective in their role as a care coordinator and patient advocate.

They also need to be aware of other relationships that need to be cultivated. These include additional individuals/groups that may facilitate or provide the resources (both human and financial) in order to **transform practice,** thus enabling those clinicians who work within the CNL's microsystem to ultimately **transform care**. (Figure 4.1)

Clinical Nurse Leaders empower their teams through team coordination and shared decision making, coaching, feedback, and encouragement and fully utilize their skills and knowledge in a relational way. With each member contributing his or her expertise toward caring for patients, together they reduce medical errors and improve safe, quality care outcomes.

They ensure all team members are linked, working together to address the needs of each patient within a cohort or group. Although the primary entry point for practice is a patient care unit or area (*i.e.*, clinical microsystem), the CNL essentially coordinates the lateral integration of care services through multiple teams and departments by

- using culturally competent, open, effective communication skills to build trust and understanding, including all team members using language and references understood by everyone else, including patients and staff from other departments;

- collaborating respectfully and positively to identify patient care needs, treatment strategies and interventions, and to evaluate the patient's progress toward discharge;

- role modeling the highest ethical and moral standards of conduct and integrity in building collegial relationships.

Figure 4.1: Transforming Practice to Transform Care

Clinical Nurse Leader	Transforming Practice	Transforming Care
Clinician at the Point of Care	Intra and Interdisciplinary Teams (Managers)	Intra and Interdisciplinary Teams (Clinicians)
Leadership & Change	Executive and Senior Leadership (Servant, Transformational Leadership) Leading across organization (macrosystems) and departments (mesosystems) Leading Lasting Change Professional Practice Council	Nurse Managers and Unit/Area Leadership (Transformational, Horizontal, Relational Leadership) Leading at point of care (microsystems) Implementing changes based on evidence and patient care outcomes
Interdisciplinary Relationships	Administrative Staff Senior Leaders Case Managers CNS Care Coordinators Physicians Informatics Educators	Lateral Integration of Care Nurse Managers Nursing Staff Case Managers CNS CNE Social Services Therapists Pharmacists Technicians Others
Knowledge Transfer	Senior Leaders Educators Professional Groups Schools and Students Committees and Councils Communities of Practice Strategic Planning Legislators	Patients and Families Point of Care Staff Graduates/New CNLs Other Professional Groups Educators Informatics Shared Governance Councils (Unit-Based Councils)
Outcomes Management	The Joint Commission and Institutes of Medicine Experts Quality Systems Staff Quality Improvement and Performance Measures Databases (National Database of Nursing Quality Indicators, NDNQI)	Direct-Care Nurses Interdisciplinary Team Members Patients and Families Risk Management Staff/Committee (RCA Reviews) Data Analysis and Systems Review Teams
Professional Development	Self Others Patients and Families Communities of Practice	Self Others Patients and Families Students/New CNLs

The debate about whether we actually need the Clinical Nurse Leader generally revolves around the roles of the CNE, CNS, and ARNP. However, when we explore their intradisciplinary relationships another question arises: Why do we need a CNL when we have a Case Manager?

The Case Management Society of America (CMSA) defines *case management* as:

"a collaborative process of assessment, planning, facilitation, and advocacy for options and services to meet an individual's health needs through communication and available resources to promote quality, cost effective outcomes" (2002, p 3).

On the surface there appears to be clear areas of overlap between the Case Manager and the CNL. A closer look reveals that it is in the way they both work that makes them *complementary* to each other rather than the same. While both share an interest in outcomes related to length of stay or re-admission rates, they approach the issue from different perspectives. The CNL looks at clinical outcomes and how to prevent secondary conditions such as infections, DVT, and other complications and delays that may extend length of stay.

The Case Manager looks at healthcare reimbursement, community resources, support needed, equipment availability, such as the wound vacuum for a patient with pressure ulcers, and how to contain costs to the organization related to unnecessary services or expenses. As the CNL assesses care pathways for the prevention of additional problems, the Case Manager works within external care pathways as determined by health insurance companies, accounting for and negotiating any extra hospital or home care time required for the patient to fully recover.

The Case Manager is a significant member of the care team. It is crucial that CNLs spend some time working with them during their orientation to better understand what they do and identify how to integrate their role into the patient's plan of care. In fact, spending time building trust and collegial relationships with all the members of the team is essential for them to "fit with the social and cultural context of the facility" (Terra 2007, p 148).

***

Failure to spend time preparing their integration into the interdisciplinary team could result in some challenges for the CNL, expressed in the form of resistance to their role.

In advocating for high quality, evidence-based practice at the point of care delivery and attempting to manage care outcomes, CNLs may inadvertently challenge the balance of how the team has been working, resulting in

- the need to maintain an already established professional identity;
- the historical "power position" and authority of medicine;
- professional jealousies, fears, and misunderstandings;
- traditional hierarchies (*i.e.*, top-down management);

- complex decision-making structures and processes traditionally associated with multi-disciplinary team activities and functions.

It is important Clinical Nurse Leaders are self aware because it is possible that they themselves may demonstrate some of these behaviors in relation to their own profession. Relational leadership plays a dynamic role in their work, which is a genuine move towards patient-focused, patient-centric care. It is not a means of shifting the power base of the group but, rather of sharing power to achieve the best possible patient care outcomes TOGETHER.

However, even in the most effective teams, interpersonal and relational conflicts occur.

Sooner or later everyone becomes involved in some form of disagreement or conflict. We work with people. People become offended, misunderstood, tired, frustrated, overworked, grieved, and vulnerable with one another when promises are broken or trust and expectations seemingly violated. Conflict is inevitable but does not have to be completely negative. It can lead to productive discussions that improve interdisciplinary communication and team effectiveness.

The key to managing conflict, while protecting relationships, lies in open, honest, caring communication. Of vital importance is the CNLs' ability to maintain a confidence with their peers and those with whom they work, resisting the temptation to label individuals as "difficult" if they have had a challenging conversation with them. Whether it be with a floor nurse expressing resistance to some change, a physician not hearing what is being said, or a therapist not understanding the CNL role, crucial conversations are going to become a part of a Clinical Nurse Leaders' daily workload. By keeping their heads (knowledge), hearts (compassion), and hands (actions) aligned with habits (practice) that respect and preserve relationships (Blanchard & Hodges, 2003), the CNL can continue maximizing opportunities for safe, evidence-based, outcomes-driven practice.

One of the Clinical Nurse Leader's most important roles is to advocate for their patients, families, team members, organizations, and themselves.

They adhere to strong ethical principles and standards of conduct when advocating for patient rights, quality outcomes, and equitable treatment and access to care. As conduits between patients and healthcare delivery and information systems, they ensure patients and families are included in care decisions.

CNLs advocate for their intra and interdisciplinary team members and the organization in various forums and political arenas, including health care reform. They interpret and defend the significance of their own and other nursing roles to policy makers, healthcare providers, and consumers when advocating for the nursing profession and quality nursing care services.

As the coordinator of care for their caseload, the CNL, alongside their intra and interdisciplinary colleagues, makes sure patients receive the best possible care with the best possible outcomes. In the event errors occur or care is less than optimum, the relationships they build will enable them to lead on discussions that reflect on events and provide solutions.

POINT TO MAGNET

Interdisciplinary relationships are about building collaborative working partnerships *in* excellence, *for* excellence in patient care outcomes. They are built and sustained with a sense of mutual respect, based on the premise that all members of the healthcare team make essential and meaningful contributions in achieving positive clinical outcomes. Clinical Nurse Leaders facilitate and engage staff in these valued relationships within and among the disciplines through horizontal leadership, shared authority, and cooperative negotiation and decision making. This facilitation and engagement can be seen in Magnet organizations who have implemented Relationship-Based Care as a professional practice model for nursing services and organizationally. They help their team members explore conflict management strategies and use crucial conversations effectively to preserve the professional and therapeutic relationships important in coordinating safe, efficient, quality, compassionate patient care.

Chapter 5:
Knowledge Transfer

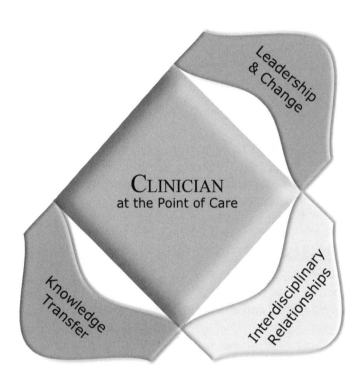

Leadership & Change

CLINICIAN
at the Point of Care

Knowledge Transfer

Interdisciplinary Relationships

As the third element of the *Transforming Practice, Transforming Care™* model for the clinician at the point of care, *knowledge transfer* is an ongoing activity that underpins the very essence of the Clinical Nurse Leader role and is perhaps the most valuable tool in changing practice through horizontal leadership.

This chapter examines the following:

1. **Who** the knowledge is transferred to
2. **What** kind of knowledge is transferred
3. **How** the knowledge is transferred
4. **The skills** required in order to effectively transfer the knowledge

Clinical Nurse Leaders work closely with well integrated, often widely diverse teams, constantly sharing their knowledge with a variety of different levels of staff and professional groups.

They share knowledge with

- physicians as they accompany them on patient rounds;
- the interdisciplinary team as they plan care for a patient;
- the unit leadership team (Charge Nurse, Nurse Manager, and CNE);
- unit-based practice council;
- risk management and quality committees;
- direct caregivers;

- patients and their families;
- professional colleagues;
- home health and long term care agencies;
- other Clinical Nurse Leaders;
- members of the shared governance committees;
- peers inside and outside of the organization.

The challenge for the CNL is knowing how to effectively and efficiently manage the knowledge and information needed to engage in the horizontal leadership and lateral integration of services.

This ensures the accurate transfer of knowledge and information to the correct people at the correct time and can be achieved by using a variety of informal and formal approaches.

Informal opportunities include

- **working with a direct caregiver at the point of care** in implementing evidence-based practice, demonstrating new technology, assessing and planning the care of their patients, particularly those who have complex needs; in fact,

  "Teaching other direct care providers how to assist clients, families and communities to be health literate and independent managers of their own care is a systems responsibility of the Clinical Nurse Leader" (AACN, 2007, p 8);

- **rounding with the medical staff**, the primary nurse, and other members of the interdisciplinary team such as therapists and pharmacists;

- *sharing information with unit-based colleagues* on new initiatives, discussing solutions to clinical challenges, presenting on the impact of their role, generating issues for practice-based evidence, and providing updates on the wider organizational objectives they are required to implement;

- *attending case management meetings* about patients within their assigned unit, particularly those with complex needs;

- *providing health promotion and discharge information* to patients and their families at the point of care;

- *documenting* in the patients' healthcare records;

- *participating in unit leadership* (Nurse Manager, Charge Nurse, and CNE) *discussions* on translating directives from the macro to the micro level and identifying approaches to implementation and evaluation.

More formal approaches to knowledge transfer include

- *presenting a case study at grand rounds* to members of the multi-disciplinary team;

- *making a formal presentation* at a conference or publishing an article on their experiences as a CNL, the challenges they have met in integrating the role in their organization, the outcomes they have influenced and improved, and, most important, how it was achieved;

- *attending a root cause analysis* (RCA) following an incident on their unit, advising on potential solutions, and implementing changes;

- *mentoring new CNL graduates* through their transition to practice by supporting, encouraging, and gently challenging them as they grow into their new role;

- *communicating through technology.*

Clinical Nurse Leaders are expected to collaborate with the broadest groups of internal and external stakeholders in coordinating care for their patient cohort. It is important to remember that their graduate and post-graduate academic education and clinical experiences are aimed at improving quality and outcomes to a more diverse and remote patient/client population than those seen in clinics and hospitals.

Having looked at the *who, what,* and *how* of knowledge transfer, there is clearly a need for the CNL to be both competent and confident in a number of different skills, including but not limited to the following:

- Coaching and feedback
- Technology
- Presentation
- Principles of adult learning

The coaching role of Clinical Nurse Leaders cannot be underestimated. It is a tool they will use in all the informal areas of information sharing and is probably

their most influential approach to changing current behavior and improving clinical outcomes within the knowledge transfer process.

Coaching can be an ideal tool for elevating team performance, improving productivity, enhancing employee autonomy, and improving organizational performance (Habel & Yoder, 2007). However, it is often confused with precepting and mentoring. Generally occurring with individuals or perhaps small groups, one of the easiest ways to define coaching is in terms of percentage of time spent on task-focused activities and the psychosocial relationship between the coach and the coachee. (Figure 5.1)

Figure 5.1: The Coaching Relationship

Coaching is NOT precepting.
Where the main focus (75%) is about achieving competency in a pre-determined series of tasks, with the relationship only forming about 25% of the process.

Coaching is NOT mentoring.
Where a long term relationship is developed that is 90% focused on the interpersonal relationship and only 10% on tasks.

Coaching is.....
A roughly equal split between task focused skills (50-60%) and the psychosocial aspect (40-50%) of the relationship.

(Habel & Yoder, 2007)

Coaching not only provides an opportunity for the transmission of knowledge on a task or process through demonstration, encouragement, and feedback, but also helps to build a relationship of trust and safety.

An integral part of the coaching process is the ability of the CNL to provide clear, concise, and supportive feedback to staff. In a world where many problems have been exacerbated through leaders and managers "sugarcoating" situations rather than dealing with the issue directly, the ability of the CNL to hold difficult conversations when necessary is a skill with which they need to be comfortable and competent.

It is often asked whether a Clinical Nurse Leader can be a preceptor to newly licensed nurses because of their advanced clinical experience.

There are two key reasons the authors caution against this:

1. The role of the CNL is to empower the direct caregivers to become more confident and accomplished in what they do. This includes developing their preceptor skills, not taking them away from them.

2. The responsibility of CNLs is to provide support to all of the staff in their units, rather than focus on one or two as they would do if they were in a preceptor role. However, they will work with many staff who are being precepted with an expectation that they may coach the new nurse in his/her growth and development as they would any other.

***

While Clinical Nurse Leaders already use an extensive network of healthcare technology within and across the macro, meso, and assigned clinical microsystems,

it is essential they understand information technology systems in order to effectively obtain knowledge and transmit it to others.

When engaging in evidence-based practice and practice-based evidence, CNLs may utilize computerized record systems, information technology, and multiple internet search engines to access the most current information available to assist in their decision making. They collaborate with other healthcare providers, patients, and family members through technologies such as email, telephone, videophone, and computer-based and fiber-optic programs. Simulation technology, advanced medical devices, and greater uses of patient care monitors in outpatient populations (*i.e.*, telemetry and telehealth) open new pathways for communicating and delivering patient care.

Likewise, CNLs measure and track data to guide their clinical judgments and to change plans of care.

They pull from epidemiological, social, and environmental data, assessing risks, evaluating potential patient care outcomes, and making recommendations to intra and interdisciplinary colleagues working within their assigned patient group.

As technology advances, so do the opportunities to expand the CNL role. One such opportunity is in the new field of telehealth.

Telehealth, like telemedicine, captures the imagination of nurses seeking new opportunities and challenges in providing care to everyone who needs it, not just those with the easiest access to traditional hospitals or clinics.

The emerging subspecialty of Telehealth Nursing Practice and how Clinical Nurse Leaders might participate in this work offers an image of knowledge transfer and outcomes management in action.

Telehealth nursing is currently a subspecialty of ambulatory care nursing. Clinical Nurse Leaders might partner with these nurse experts in coordinating care for their unique patient populations to improve clinical outcomes, particularly those in underserviced areas. The American Academy of Ambulatory Care Nursing has developed a network of telehealth standards of practice, resources, education, and the Telehealth Nursing Practice Special Interest Group. Currently, groups are working on how to improve clinical practice and quality outcomes, educate nurses in telehealth, and communicate and network with one another around issues related to telehealth in practice.

As has already been identified in the how of knowledge transfer, CNLs are required to be competent in a variety of presentation formats to meet the needs of the diverse groups with whom they will share knowledge.

While it goes without saying that preparation is the key, we have already determined that a comfort level with "working on the fly" is necessary in this role, particularly when they are required to present to a committee or grand round at short notice. As long as they remember to

- talk to the audience, not to the white board or the power point screen;
- avoid putting too much text on a slide (the audience will not be able to read it anyway);
- stay relevant to the subject;
- *avoid reading the slides to the audience;*
- stay within the allocated time;
- speak clearly and objectively;

they will be seen as professional and actively engage their audiences.

Additionally, CNLs may present on a more informal basis at unit meetings to nursing colleagues and/or members of the interdisciplinary team. Possible presentations may include providing feedback on action to be taken following a systems-based clinical incident or celebrating successes achieved in the unit on their collaborative approaches to patient care outcomes.

The presentation may resemble an informal group conversation but still needs to be structured and easily followed. Whenever possible, being mindful of HIPPA regulations, a prepared handout with at least a few salient bullet points for discussion often helps maintain the flow of the interaction. These informal presentations frequently relax and engage staff in active problem solving. This demonstrates to the team the CNL is a good listener and recognizes his or her way is not the only way to accomplish the same patient-centric outcomes.

Understanding the principles of adult learning (androgogy) is vital to the successful transference of knowledge in whatever situation the Clinical Nurse Leader may function.

All adults learn best when motivated by a need to know, and when they see an immediate application of new knowledge to their practice. Adults retain information longer when they receive it through a variety of different approaches including visual, kinesthetic, and auditory; for example, showing a video or watching a demonstration of CPR training and then performing the activity (the watch-then-practice approach). These techniques of accelerated learning will serve the CNL well. However, it must be emphasized they also need to transfer knowledge to patients and their families, which requires the ability to communicate in language easily understood by non-healthcare professionals.

Additionally, there are some techniques to consider when educating patients who are seniors:

- They generally learn best when the information has a relevance to them, either now or in their past. For instance, if they have cancer and a friend had a similar cancer and was cured through a particular treatment, they will be much more positive and open to the information they are receiving than if their friend had a poor outcome.

- They may require larger print on any health promotion or information materials because of age-related variances in their visual acuity.

- They may be unable to read and are embarrassed to admit this. Therefore, any materials provided to the older patient are best developed in picture format with minimal written information.

The ability to read and process information is an important consideration when patients receive medication on discharge, as one orange container looks the same as the next one, where mistakes can potentially result in re-admission. It is the CNL's responsibility to work with the direct caregiver, patient, family, and pharmacist to avoid this potential occurrence.

***

Clinical Nurse Leaders have an obligation to update themselves about any national and organizational healthcare initiatives and issues pertinent to the macro, meso, and microsystems in which they work. In other words, they need to set aside time for environmental scanning.

To help facilitate this, CNLs need to develop a communication feedback loop early in acquiring their role, so they are clear from where they receive their knowledge and to whom they need to transmit it. (Figure 5.2)

While this model will differ depending upon the clinical environment in which they practice, it provides an ideal tool for CNLs to

- identify who they need to build a relationship with;
- plan who they need to meet as they orientate in their new role;

Figure 5.2: Communication Feedback Loop

- enable them to visualize how their role will function within their clinical microsytem, while being strongly connected to the goals of the organization.

One of the biggest challenges for Clinical Nurse Leaders is in adapting to the language of the 'Cs' (Chief Nursing Officer, Chief Executive Officer, Chief Financial Officer) when preparing reports for executive levels.

Executive leaders require feedback that is short, to the point, and outcomes-focused. They have little time and, generally, will only read the executive summary of a report, often just before attending the meeting. The CNL should not be concerned when politely asked to *cut to the chase*. Executives wear many hats and have little time to address any of them in detail. Their concern, while often seen in fiscal terms and outcomes, is to provide the best quality care for the patient in a safe and healthy environment. That is how they will ensure the future of the facility.

Bringing others into the emerging and rapidly developing world of these advanced generalists in nursing through education and mentoring enables healthcare leaders to realize new possibilities for the CNL to impact social and health care reform, build new professional partnerships, and explore new knowledge, innovations, and improvements, transforming practice at the point of care.

POINT TO MAGNET

Nurses around the world celebrate Florence Nightingale's birthday (May 12) during Nurses' Week every year. Her vision firmly established and mobilized a profession. Clinical Nurse Leaders join nurse researchers, leaders, educators, clinicians, and students in advancing that profession into the next generation and beyond through technology and horizontal leadership at the point of care delivery for patient groups, families, and their team members.

Nightingale exemplified the intent of the ANCC Magnet Recognition Program® in everything she did for nursing. Committed to knowledge, innovation, and improvements in professional nursing and patient care outcomes, she built the Nightingale School to train nurses and define the content and context of their education. She, too, believed that strong leadership, empowered professionals, and exemplary practice served as essential building blocks for exceptional (*i.e.*, Magnet-recognized) organizations, but not as the final goals. Clinical Nurse Leaders have an ethical and professional responsibility to contribute to patient care, the organization, and the profession in terms of new knowledge, innovations, and improvements. They must participate in redesigning and redefining healthcare's current systems and practices through knowledge transfer and advances in technology.

Clinical Nurse Leader:
Transforming Practice, Transforming Care

Chapter 6:
Outcomes Management

While *Clinical Nurse Leaders (CNLs) are differentiated* **through their position** *at* **the point of care, their purpose is clearly** *defined* **by the outcomes they achieve.**

In fact, it is this fourth element of the *Transforming Practice, Transforming Care™* model, *outcomes management,* that provides the best justification for the role's introduction, expansion, and continuity as nurse executives seek to obtain support to fund CNL positions by articulating their return on investment (ROI) to the organization through

- increased/improved intra and interdisciplinary communication;
- reduced medical errors and sentinel events;
- increased recruitment/retention;
- increased staff job satisfaction;
- decreased patient complaints;
- increased patient satisfaction;
- safe, cost effective care.

To be most effective in outcomes management, Clinical Nurse Leaders require specialized knowledge and skills in three areas:

- An understanding of the outcomes they measure and why/how the data is important for managing patient care delivery
- The availability of tools to help them ensure that their interventions and outcomes are

based on evidence and the most current research

- How to use best practices, techniques, and approaches to influence patient care outcomes

With so many Clinical Nurse Leaders working in acute care, it is easily forgotten when discussing outcomes that (1) the CNL role has a proactive, as well as reactive, role, (2) has equal responsibilities and accountabilities for health promotion and illness intervention, and (3) can be found in any healthcare environment, including long term care, home health care, primary, and acute care. While the application and systems may be different, the core skills and knowledge needed to perform their duties are the same.

While their role in outcomes management brings them into contact with different departments, such as risk management and quality, a recent study conducted by Joint Commission and the Robert Wood Foundation identified that novice nurses felt they were poorly prepared or had little, if any, understanding of their role in quality improvement (QI) (Kovner et al, 2010). This finding has clear implications for the direction and justification of CNL roles, as their work provides them with endless opportunities to educate and empower their nursing colleagues in the process, purpose, and importance of performance measures and outcomes management at the point of care delivery where it is most relevant.

Clinical Nurse Leaders work with a variety of other professionals, as well as their intra and interdisciplinary teams, in identifying WHAT clinical measures need to be addressed and HOW clinical outcomes can be improved.

The **WHAT** includes

- core measures;
- benchmarks such as the National Database of Nursing Quality Indicators (NDNQI);
- clinical concerns arising from patient and family complaints;
- potential risks identified through the introduction of new technologies, equipment, treatment regimens, or medication therapies (AACN, 2007);
- actual incidents or near misses, such as the "right drug, wrong patient";
- discharge planning and re-admission rates;
- Joint Commission, Agency for Healthcare Administration AHCA, or Occupational Safety and Health Administration (OSHA) goals;
- patterns of concern (*e.g.* sudden increase in the incidence of urinary tract infections);
- preventable conditions or "never events";
- concerns raised by clinicians in practice;
- practice-based evidence related to quality, safety, and competency issues;
- organizational goals (reduction in medication errors, falls, improvement in Press Ganey percentiles);
- impact of continuing education programs, mandatory education, and in-services.

The **HOW** involves influencing the way care is provided and implementing evidence-based practice at the point at which it is delivered. This requires a toolkit of skills and approaches to influence and measure patient care outcomes including

- communicating effectively within their teams;
- creating an environment that is safe to ask questions;
- developing an ability to understand the systems within their organizations, how they can affect patient outcomes, and how they can be changed;
- synthesizing data and using it to effect care delivery and patient outcomes
- understanding how to implement evidence-based practice (EBP) and practice-based evidence (PBE).

1. Communicating effectively within their teams.

The CNL's team consists of five separate groups, all of whom are inter-related through their core purpose of providing safe, quality-driven, direct and indirect care to individual patients and their families. These groups consist of

- nurses who provide the direct care to patients that fall within the scope of the CNL's caseload;
- the unit leadership team (Nurse Manager, Charge Nurse, and CNE);
- the interdisciplinary team (involved with the provision of the care to patients in the CNL's caseload);
- wider teams associated with organizational goals of providing safe patient care driven by quality outcomes, safety, and protecting public health and well being, such as the safety/quality/risk departments;
- the mesosystem of the service or department the CNL works in (e.g., Department of

Nursing/Patient Care Services) which translates the goals and vision of the macrosystem.

Facilitating accurate communication among staff of all levels and disciplines within these five groups is an essential requisite for CNLs and perhaps one of the biggest areas in which they can influence patient care outcomes. Therefore, they must be confident in their ability to tackle challenging clinical situations calmly, assertively, and professionally. They must also be comfortable in role modeling these behaviors to their nursing colleagues.

One of the key duties within their role as horizontal leaders is helping their immediate nursing and interdisciplinary team members move to action and results rather than ignoring, blaming, or reflecting anger or conflict. The study entitled *Silence Kills: The Seven Crucial Conversations for Healthcare* (Maxfield et al, 2005) stated that

- 84% of physicians and 62% of nurses and other clinical caregivers observed co-workers taking shortcuts that were potentially harmful to patients;
- 88% of physicians and 48% of nurses and other clinical caregivers work with people who show poor clinical judgment in providing care;
- less than 10% of clinical staff confront colleagues about their observations or concerns;
- one in five physicians report seeing patients actually harmed by their silence;

- the 10% who speak out about their concerns see better patient care outcomes and are generally more satisfied in their jobs.

Clearly, an awareness of the consequences of NOT advocating for their patients, addressing clinical issues as they arise, or following their nursing and CNL professional codes and standards of conduct is vital for the Clinical Nurse Leader.

The theory of holding these difficult conversations surrounding patient outcomes, rather than stumbling over personalities and/or egos, needs to be learned and taught. While some CNLs will feel more confident in their ability to address these challenges, for others the practice of holding these crucial conversations and learning how to manage conflict through preparation and compassion, while respecting and preserving relationships, needs to be a high priority in their ongoing professional development.

2. Creating an environment that is safe to ask questions.

Change and the integration of evidence-based practice in clinical microsystems can only occur in environments where staff feel safe to ask what they may feel are *stupid questions*. It is important for the CNL to recognize their colleagues and peers learn in different ways and sometimes get distracted, not always "getting it" the first time. When CNLs share their experiences with new staff by describing how they have learned from them, they can make direct caregivers more comfortable and willing to take risks in order to achieve a positive patient outcome. Two examples of such crucial conversations are confronting a colleague about something they should have done or calling the doctor back when they are not happy with the outcome of the call.

Sharing their experiences does not mean, however, that the CNL should wear their *hearts on their sleeves*. It means they maintain a caring and accessible professionalism with appropriate boundaries for contributing to a safe learning, practice environment. Building collegial relationships in this way

- helps take away some of the perceptions that other staff may hold about CNLs being clinical elitists;
- provides the CNL with opportunities to discuss the rationale for certain activities;
- opens up discussions to ideas and innovations staff may have felt uneasy expressing;
- strengthens the team as mutual respect is developed.

3. **Developing an ability to understand the systems within their organizations, how they can affect patient outcomes, and how they can be changed.**

Over the years there has been a shift in attitude away from blaming the individual clinician for every clinical incident or medical error toward recognizing many can be attributed to a systems error. In order for them to be proactive in their role of promoting patient safety and improving patient outcomes, Clinical Nurse Leaders need to have an understanding of

- the organization's structures, processes, mechanisms, and goals for addressing incidents that occur through systems errors;

- the process of investigating a clinical incident and identifying a systems error;
- the best way to raise concerns when they identify potential risks;
- developing solutions through rapid process improvement groups and their role in implementing the change.

These are important competencies for CNLs and ones that can be achieved through close collaboration with their Nurse Manager and staff from the quality and risk management departments.

4. Synthesizing data and using it to effect care delivery and patient outcomes.

While it is not intended CNLs sit at computers all day inputting data or being unusually adept in the use of advanced computer programs, they do need some skills and abilities in the area of information and computer technology. They will work with direct care staff to collect and synthesize data into meaningful conclusions for their clinical areas to inform and guide practice and care delivery.

They identify the processes by which data is being collected from their assigned units to the organizational (macro) level and need to clearly address measures they monitor. Some organizations will have a clear vision about specific targets they want the CNL to impact, such as

- length of stay;
- re-admission rates;
- patient flow;
- nurse retention;

- core measures;
- preventable events.

Other targets will be more unit-focused, such as the incidence of post-operative wound infections, medication errors, fall rates, and discharge delays.

5. **Understanding how to implement evidence-based practice (EBP) and practice-based evidence (PBE).**

The models of evidence-based practice, research-based evidence, and practice-based evidence referenced throughout this book are central to the delivery of clinically effective care and are some of the strongest tools CNLs have in their repertoire. The ANCC (2008) defines these models in their Components and Sources of Evidence for the Magnet Recognition Program® as follows:

- *Evidence-based practice (EBP)* is a science to service model "for the conscientious use/integration of the best research evidence with clinical expertise and patient preferences in nursing practice" (p 39) to deliver cost effective care.

- *Research-based evidence (RBE)* is translated into evidence-based practice, which is then incorporated into practice-based learning and improvement.

- *Practice-based evidence (PBE)* is a practice to science model "in which data are derived from interventions thought to be effective but for which empirical evidence is lacking." (p 40)

It is no longer regarded as acceptable to change practice on what appears to be a good idea or which has been based on tradition.

Not only does the CNL need to understand the principles of change management to achieve better outcomes, but must also have an advanced competency in managing complex data based on evidence and research. Professional and ethical inquiry enables them to question the status quo without criticizing negatively and making people feel threatened or discounted. Their critical reasoning skills need to be well honed to make accurate clinical judgments around the data and clinical measures.

Much of the evidence driving their care decisions will be provided to them in the form of policies and/or procedures they may or may not have been part in developing. They need the skills to understand and effectively critique the research and evidence behind them and embed these in recommendations for implementing changes.

PBE enables the Clinical Nurse Leader to raise questions about current practice, study the evidence and current research available, and plan strategies to move forward either within their own microsystems or organizationally. After identifying an area of concern/practice, they will assess what has traditionally worked (PBE) and what new approaches/treatments show evidence of being more effective (EBP). Then, they will decide if this is a practice or systems issue and determine what interventions will yield the best patient outcomes.

It is important to note here that while CNLs work in their own assigned microsystems, they need to be networked within their organization to facilitate communication and information sharing. Working in silos must be avoided at all costs to protect patients and the public. For example, an increase in UTIs or wound infections that reaches far beyond one CNL's unit can be more effectively and efficiently stopped with collegial engagement in shared decision making and rapid intervention at the meso and/or macrosystem levels, depending on how far the issue has spread. They also need to be able to share what they have learned within their own microsystems with colleagues in order to influence practice in other clinical areas.

One of the tools that can help traverse the theory-practice gap and bring evidence to the point of care delivery is through a process called a clinical audit. (Figure 6.1)

Not to be confused with the data collected for Minimum Data Set (MDS), a *clinical audit* provides a *systematic approach* to implementing clinical evidence to practice, then identifying where change is required in order to maximize improvement in clinical outcomes.

There are 7 stages to a well designed clinical audit:

1. *Identify the practice to be audited (e.g., the compliance of prophylactic measures to reduce DVT in an orthopedic unit).*

Figure 6.1: A Model for the Clinical Audit Process

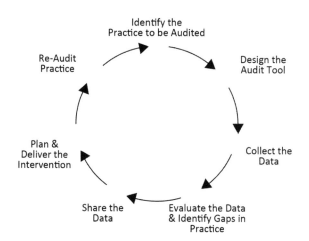

2. *Design the audit tool,* which may be based upon an existing protocol in the facility, or if this does not exist, examining the evidence and developing key points of measuring practice, such as compliance to passive leg exercises, deep breathing, administration times of medications, etc.

3. *Collect the data* through formal and informal observation of clinical practice and review of clinical records.

4. *Evaluate the data and identify gaps in practice* by measuring the results against the evidence underpinning the audit tool.

5. *Share the data* with the appropriate healthcare workers, obtain their feedback, and discuss potential solutions. This is a crucial stage in change management and an ideal way to engage staff in the process.

6. *Plan and deliver the intervention* that may be conducted over several units. Therefore, the CNLs

involved will liaise with each other and identify a collaborative way to move forward. At this point, the CNE, Unit/Nurse Managers, CNS, and members of the interdisciplinary team (where appropriate) will be engaged in a collaborative approach to identify the solutions and the staff education to improve the outcomes.

7. *Re-audit practice* to measure the effectiveness of the education, both formal and informal, and of compliance to the change if one was made.

This method can be used to

- evaluate the compliance to core measures;
- track problems with discharge planning;
- identify reasons for increased length of stay;
- measure compliance to a new policy or procedure;
- help clinicians answer questions that arise from clinical practice.

A clinical audit provides an ideal way to apply EBP to any workplace or practice setting. It is an excellent opportunity for one–on–one teaching in the clinical area. By engaging the staff in the process and the subsequent discussion of the results, the importance of their role in quality improvement at the point of care becomes clear to them.

One of the most empowering ways CNLs can help direct caregivers increase their knowledge of the quality process, and subsequently take more responsibility and accountability for the services they provide to their patients, is to involve them in the clinical audit process, including auditing each other's practice. In order for them to have the time to do this, the authors suggest that for a period of no more than two hours the CNL takes over the direct caregiver's caseload. This provides opportunities for the CNL to

- focus time to work with their assigned patient populations and their families;
- assess record keeping and other aspects of the care delivery process;
- connect relationally with their interdisciplinary team members.

POINT TO MAGNET

CNLs contribute significantly to the Magnet journey in their organizations by demonstrating how nursing makes a difference in outcomes management for patients and patient populations. The Magnet model modified in 2008 emphasizes the criticality of managing and sustaining empirical quality outcomes, one of five key components of nursing excellence in providing patient care. Clinical Nurse Leaders help empower staff when they participate with them in shared governance, a management model which enables the direct care nurse to have a stronger voice in how patient care is delivered and clinical outcomes are managed. CNLs work closely with the rest of the healthcare team and the unit-based practice councils for their assigned microsystems. They teach, coach, guide, and fold their empirical outcomes into presentations for other nursing governance councils, *e.g.,* Quality or Research Councils and interdisciplinary teams.

Clinical Nurse Leader:
Transforming Practice, Transforming Care

Chapter 7:
Clinician at the Point of Care

The previous four elements of the *Transforming Practice, Transforming Care™* model have highlighted the areas of skill and knowledge required by Clinical Nurse Leaders for them to function effectively as clinicians at the point of care. Interestingly, it is this aspect of the role that has caused much confusion for Nurse Managers and executive nurses. This has resulted in some CNLs leaving the role because they have been unable to practice their advanced generalist functions to effect patient care outcomes in the way the role is intended. Before going any further, it is important to answer two questions frequently asked about the CNL role:

1. Where is the Clinical Nurse Leader's point of care delivery?
2. What constitutes a Clinical Nurse Leader's assigned caseload?

Where is the Clinical Nurse Leader's point of care delivery?

They work in a variety of clinical areas, including acute care, long term care, home health care, telehealth, rehabilitation, and primary care. While this diversity of practice settings makes it difficult to determine an exact model for each clinical area, the location of the *point of care* can always be determined by

- the assigned unit/microsystem where they practice, such as a Medical/Surgical unit, doctor's office, or an outpatient facility;
- the caseload/patient population or cohort for which they are accountable.

What constitutes a Clinical Nurse Leader's assigned caseload?

The question of *what is a caseload* is perhaps the most difficult concept for other healthcare providers and colleagues to grasp. A Clinical Nurse Leader's caseload is generally defined by their assigned work units, microsystems, and/or patient population served. While a direct caregiver might be allocated a group of two to six patients depending on the type of clinical unit or environment of care they work in and which may be even higher depending on their shift, the CNL's cohort group may include as many as twenty or more patients, depending on the size of their clinical microsystem.

The caseload for a CNL, therefore, is defined as an assignment comprised of all the patients within an allocated unit/environment.

In an **acute care unit,** the caseload could range from twenty to forty patients. Some of the larger clinical units, therefore, have chosen to introduce more than one CNL, each having an equal allocation of patients whose care they coordinate and oversee.

In the **community,** a caseload may include all the patients within a defined geographical area.

In an **outpatient clinic,** the caseload might extend to include any person who attends the clinic.

In **long term care,** the caseload may be an individual wing or the whole facility, depending on its size.

No matter which area CNLs practice, they must know about every patient within their caseload, establish a therapeutic and caring relationship with each one and their families, and remain current with any changes in their care as they progress towards or maintain health. This means building up and sustaining excellent communication and collaboration links with direct caregivers and other healthcare professionals.

Unfortunately, there have been many occasions reported of CNLs receiving more traditional patient assignments during times of short staffing, even on a routine basis in some organizations. Not only is this demoralizing for them (unless it is a genuine time of crisis), it diminishes their ability to meet the needs of their own patient populations whose care outcomes they manage.

This misinterpretation of what constitutes a CNL's caseload may be due to a lack of knowledge or understanding of the functional aspects of the role by Nurse Managers, Charge Nurses, and other healthcare professionals. The clarification of the role and education of colleagues are critical parts of the natural evolution and implementation of this change if it is to be firmly embedded into the clinical practice structure. In fact, CNLs should

- facilitate their own enculturation into their communities of practice;
- make visible their support from Chief Nursing Officers;

- expand others' appreciation of their contributions through

1. meetings;
2. rounding with treatment teams;
3. mentoring nurses interested in this advanced generalist role;
4. teaching, coaching, and modeling their unique role in patient care.

While we have identified the **WHERE** *and* **WHAT** *of the point of care delivery and defined the Clinical Nurse Leader's caseload, two questions still remain:*

1. How does this translate to clinical practice within an assigned microsystem?

2. How do CNLs incorporate into their clinical practice the skills and knowledge identified in the previous four elements of the *Transforming Practice, Transforming Care™* model:

   - Leadership and Change
   - Interdisciplinary Relationships
   - Knowledge Transfer
   - Outcomes Management

The majority of Clinical Nurse Leader roles have been established within the acute care sector, where they may be found in any single clinical unit, including medical/surgical units, orthopedics, pediatrics, emergency departments, operating rooms, intensive care units, primary care, and outpatient clinics. However, there is an increasing number being introduced in other areas and this will undoubtedly continue over the next few years.

While the clinical structures and functions may vary from unit to unit or system to system, the core elements of the role are the same, with communication and collaboration being the most powerful requisites for success at the point of care delivery.

Clinical Nurse Leaders have a unique position within their assigned unit, as they oversee the integration of care for every patient in their cohort from admission to discharge.

They can be instrumental in instilling confidence in families who may be concerned by the quality of care provided to their loved ones and their safety from infections, other nosocomial events, and medical errors.

To achieve this confidence, they carefully review the care plans, complete chart audits, and collaborate with healthcare team members to understand their patients' care needs and interventions, ensure care provided meets the standards tied to core measures and other desired clinical outcomes, and round on patients daily to build trusting relationships with patients and their families. In this way, CNLs can have positive outcomes on patient satisfaction, decreased lengths of stay, and improved resources utilization for point of care delivery (Ott et al, 2009).

Communication between nurses and physicians has always been a challenge. While nurses often feel medical staff do not take the time to listen to them, physicians complain nurses never seem to know their patients and frequently hear, "it is my first day back after days off" or even more frustrating "it's not my patient."

Rounding with the physician (and whenever possible, the patient's allocated nurse) is an ideal way of ensuring all information is passed to them and guaranteeing patient outcomes are not effected by inadequate communication. As relationships grow, the CNL may coordinate, and even lead, the interdisciplinary team rounds. Rounding helps build relationships of mutual respect between the two professional groups. In fact, it is a good way of developing a culture wherein not only do nurses feel more comfortable and empowered to approach physicians day-to-day but to ask questions about a particular order or another aspect of the patient's care, as well.

Rounding can be a wonderful opportunity for Clinical Nurse Leaders to fulfill their advocacy role and, when necessary, have those crucial conversations to ensure the team members are basing care on evidence-based outcomes. They can work with the direct caregivers to make changes to the patient's plan of care (which they are empowered to do as part of their role) and act as a liaison with these caregivers, informing them of any changes to the care plan. Not only does this improve communication and role models the behavior required for evolving collegial professional relationships, it helps reduce the stress and frustration of direct care nurses when they feel they are being pulled in all directions and cannot give their best to anything. Rounding with nurses and encouraging them to provide feedback to the physician through interdisciplinary rounds is an ideal mentoring opportunity.

The Clinical Nurse Leader is ideally placed to implement new ways of working to improve communication and patient and family participation.

In one Florida hospital, the introduction of bedside report was led by the CNL who role modeled the behaviors and interactions with the patient and families and worked with the direct caregivers to help them overcome their initial resistance and discomfort to the change (Sherman et al, 2009).

It should not be forgotten, however, that the Clinical Nurse Leader has a role as a direct caregiver.

Outside of their coaching role and routine interactions with patients and their families this direct caregiver role is focused on patients who have *complex needs*.

Part of the CNLs' education at an advanced level includes the completion of modules that teach advanced health care assessment and pharmacology skills. These modules provide a stronger foundation to critically reason and intervene at a level beyond that of the average nurse. This additional knowledge and higher-level competency prepares them to

- assess, plan, diagnose (within the parameters of their scope of practice), and intervene in patient care delivery and outcomes management;
- change the care plans of their assigned patient populations;
- supervise/oversee point of care delivery;
- support the direct care nurses assigned to each patient, developing them in their critical thinking skills and clinical judgments;
- make referrals to other members of the interdisciplinary team as appropriate.

It is important to remember, however, that working with patients who require a complex level of care, discharge, etc. does not constitute a clinical caseload, and those patients will still have a designated nurse providing and delivering their care. The CNL just works alongside and with them in required situations .

Even though they may be new to working as advanced generalists, the CNL's clinical skills are expected to be strong. A Clinical Nurse Leader should be functioning at least at the competent level of clinical practice as described by Benner (1984) and preferably at the proficient or advanced levels, in order for them to readily step into their more expanded duties.

Several other ways the Clinical Nurse Leader functions as a clinician at the point of care in an acute care setting have been discussed within this book including

- working with members of the interdisciplinary teams through the forum of case management meetings;
- working closely with the Case Manager to ensure outcomes are met with regard to discharge planning and re-admission rates;
- liaising with other members of the unit leadership team in identifying ways to meet organizational and unit specific outcomes;
- implementing EBP at the point of care delivery and generating questions that lead to the development of practice-based evidence, quality improvements, and new research;
- providing proactive and reactive health care activities with patients and their families.

Flexibility and adaptability are two key qualities required of CNLs, as the world of healthcare continues to change around them. This may include the type of care delivery systems in which they work.

Some facilities have moved away from the more traditional approach of patients being transferred from different floors throughout their acute care stay, to one in which they remain in the same room for the duration of their stay. Known as the acuity-adaptable model, this approach increases patient satisfaction, reduces bottlenecks caused by the flow of patients in the facility, improves patient/nurse relationships, reduces patient falls, and reduces medical errors (Hendrich et al, 2004). This model requires the CNL to have a broader knowledge base of the patient care continuum, as they will be working with a mix of high and low acuity patients. Subsequently, the clinical outcomes they are required to oversee will be more diverse. They are in an ideal position to assist with the implementation of this approach by supporting the direct caregivers in making the transition.

However, the Clinical Nurse Leader role goes beyond the needs of the acute care sector and has an equally important place in home health care.

While their caseload may be more geographically dispersed, the principles of practice for community-based or home health care CNLs are the same as in other settings. They are there to ensure safe, effective, outcomes-driven care. Their communication networks need to be powerful and reliable, and they will need to invest a good amount of time in building relationships with the interdisciplinary team members involved with the care of their patient cohorts, who may be very geographically dispersed.

Described as

"a catalyst in community healthcare transformation" *(Edouard-Trevathan, 2010, p 25),*

the Clinical Nurse Leader has a clearly identified role in supporting primary care

"to reverse the epidemic of overweight, obesity, and associated chronic diseases through coordinated multidisciplinary efforts grounded in evidence-based practice."(p 26)

Their clinical microsystems consist of those intra and interdisciplinary team members who form the nexus of the healthcare providers working with a specific cohort of patients. The location of the service may be spread over several localities within a geographical area. As with home health care, communication and collegiality are essential to effective, efficient working team practices. The targeted outcomes to be monitored and managed need to be identified and a process selected for their implementation.

As more people obtain health insurance over the coming years, it is clear that this environment is one in which the Clinical Nurse Leader has a strong future and where they can make a real difference in the quality of care provided to those who have already been exposed, either personally or through family members, to some of the health conditions prevalent today. For example, Type 2 diabetes is a critical area of health promotion and disease prevention and management in which the emerging CNL can play a key role, as healthcare services are transformed to meet the needs of this ever growing patient population.

One of the ways in which the CNL can function in a non-acute setting is within the Primary Care Medical Home (PCMH) model. Described by Strenger (2007), it provides the following to its patients:

- A continuous relationship with a physician
- A multidisciplinary team, collectively responsible for providing for a patient's longitudinal health needs and making appropriate referrals to other providers
- Coordination and integration with other providers, as well as public health and other community services, supported by health information technology
- An expanded focus on quality and safety
- Enhanced access through extended hours, open scheduling, and/or email or phone visits

It is an environment ideally suited to the Clinical Nurse Leader and one pertinent in maintaining safe, outcomes-driven practice in a new era of healthcare reform.

While the approaches that have been identified in acute care are just as applicable in the long term care sector, there are some specific areas in the latter that the CNL can influence.

One of these approaches is the introduction of regular rounding by the Clinical Nursing Assistants. A study conducted on the use of call lights by patients on twenty-seven units in fourteen hospitals demonstrated one to two hourly rounding on patients increased patient satisfaction scores, decreased falls, and reduced the number of call lights by 38% (Studer, 2004). While the research was conducted in a hospital setting where acuities and skill mix differ from long term care, the CNL would be ideally placed to work with the Clinical Nursing Assistants, using this approach as one way to improve resident outcomes.

CNLs in long term care work with all levels of nursing staff, not just those who are licensed. They ensure the facility meets the clinical standards required by OSHA, ACHA, Joint Commission, and other regulating agencies in providing a safe environment for patients, residents, and staff.

Unlike acute care, they are likely to be accountable to the Director of Nursing and may receive their organizational goals from a head office in a different location or state. But like their acute care colleagues, they need to develop close working relationships with the members of the intra and interdisciplinary teams, patients, and their families to be effective.

***

Regardless of the assigned clinical microsystem, it is important Clinical Nurse Leaders do not get caught up with attending meeting after meeting or becoming distracted by other activities that take them away from their primary accountabilities for improving patient safety and care outcomes at the point of care delivery.

While it is very relevant to the purpose of their role to share their successes, challenges, concerns, and opinions, they must work with Nurse Managers and other senior nurses within the unit/environment of care, ensuring their input into committees such as risk, safety, and quality improvement, without necessarily being present at every one.

Common practice challenges can be shared with these groups through multiple communication pathways. These pathways establish patterns for moving an identified risk and solution from the micro to the meso and macro levels whenever appropriate. Achieving this balance and avoiding duplication of effort is essential for the CNL role to work and be differentiated from other healthcare providers.

POINT TO MAGNET

CNLs are clinicians at the point of care who engage in exemplary professional practice, another key component of the Magnet Recognition Program®. They laterally integrate services across systems when working with nurses, interdisciplinary team members, professional partners, patients, and families.

They employ varied care delivery systems to promote continuous, efficient, effective, safe, and accountable care at the point of delivery, which is adapted to regulatory parameters and ethical considerations. They make accurate clinical judgments for providing care based on the unique needs, culture, and attributes of their assigned patient populations and their families. Furthermore, they are grounded by a culture of safety, quality care outcomes monitoring and management, and quality improvement through engaged participation in safety initiatives incorporating national benchmarks and best practices.

These clinicians reflect Magnet at all levels of service. They collect and analyze data, compare their outcomes to national benchmarks, *e.g.*, the National Database for Nursing Quality Indicators (NDNQI), and adapt patient care plans according to changes in patient care needs. These clinicians are uniquely positioned for transforming practice at the point of care delivery and demonstrating excellence in professional practice.

Chapter 8:
Professional Development

Outcomes Management

Leadership & Change

Professional

Development

CLINICIAN
at the Point of Care

Development

Professional

Knowledge Transfer

Interdisciplinary Relationships

Clinical Nurse Leaders have two Professional Development goals:

1. To ensure their own professional development needs are met.
2. To assist in the professional development needs of those with whom they work.

The *Transforming Practice, Transforming Care™* model for the clinician at the point of care recognizes that unlike the other five elements of the model which can be seen as separate parts of the same entity, *Professional Development* is a thread that runs throughout and cannot be separated.

Before identifying their own professional development needs, CNLs need to understand what skills they require to be effective in this aspect of their role.

While the foundation will have been laid through the completion of their master's degree based upon the program competences and required clinical experience as determined by the AACN (2007), the realities of applying these into practice may be very different. Therefore, there are other skills that may not have been apparent in the educational setting that require additional learning.

The table on page 102 (Figure 8.1) identifies the skills and competencies required of the Clinical Nurse Leader based upon the five elements of the *Transforming*

Practice, Transforming Care™ model that have been previously discussed. Along with the information in this chapter, it provides a suitable framework upon which any organization can begin to develop a role description for their new Clinical Nurse Leaders.

Based on the information in Figure 8.1 Clinical Nurse Leaders need to ask themselves, "What are the gaps in my knowledge and skills, and how am I going to fill them?"

To be effective in their roles as advanced generalists and clinical leaders, they must be able to work within healthcare settings and microsystems comprised of multiple providers, varied patient populations, and interdisciplinary team members with diverse levels of academic preparation and experience.

Also, they are required to learn new theories, concepts, advances in clinical skills and knowledge, technologies, and approaches to team and organizational effectiveness to achieve safe, outcomes-driven clinical practice.

The best way this can be achieved is through the process and application of *Lifelong Learning* defined as,

the ongoing pursuit of new knowledge and skills that develop an individual in their personal and professional life.

Many Clinical Nurse Leaders will already be comfortable with the concept of lifelong learning, and it is unlikely they will have taken the first step to becoming a CNL unless they had already "bought into" the concept. It is

Figure 8.1: *Transforming Practice, Transforming Care™*
Skill Set for the Clinician at the Point of Care

Leadership & Change	• Horizontal leadership • Transformational leadership • Situational leadership • Strategic planning • Communication across organizations at multiple levels • Micro, meso, and macrosystems interrelatedness • Change management theory and application
Interdisciplinary Relationships	• Lateral integration of care (Care coordinator) • Interprofessional partnerships • Interdisciplinary teams • Team building • Building and sustaining relationships • Conflict management
Knowledge Transfer	• Adult learning theory • Documentation and presentation skills • Coaching and feedback skills • Mentoring skills • Building professional portfolios • Environmental scanning • Research and literature review • Creating an environment for safe learning
Outcomes Management	• Clinical audits • Chart reviews • Quality systems analysis • Empirical outcomes and data management • Dashboards and scorecards • Data collection, analysis, and application to practice • Benchmarking with national databases

Clinician at the Point of Care	• Care delivery systems and models
	• Professional practice models
	• Systems theory
	• Evidence-based practice
	• Practice-based evidence
	• Reflective practice
	• Peer reviews
	• Care of patients with complex needs

important to realize, however, even though they have just completed the graduate program, they will be presented with many challenges as their role is introduced in the organization, no matter how experienced they are.

It is perhaps appropriate at this time to consider the discussion on whether or not the CNL is an advanced practice role. If not, then why are they required to complete a master's degree program that includes higher level health assessment skills and the lateral integration of care delivery services?

The Institute of Medicine (2003) reported in the *Health Professions Education: A Bridge to Quality* that in order to best meet patients' needs

"all health professionals [i.e., Clinical Nurse Leaders] should be educated to deliver patient-centered care as members of an interdisciplinary team, emphasizing evidence-based practice, quality improvement approaches, and informatics." (p 3)

With one of the elements of the CNL role being to provide horizontal leadership to other nurses and members of the interdisciplinary team at the point of care, their level of preparation for this work is justifiably beyond that of a baccalaureate degree. To improve patient safety and clinical outcomes, it is necessary for CNLs to build upon the clinical skills they have already gained as direct caregivers, with the addition of advanced theory and clinical underpinnings, which are crucial to meeting the responsibilities and accountabilities of their role.

Benner et al (2010) discussed four shifts in thinking that need to occur in all nursing education, but which specifically apply to how CNLs approach their professional development within their practice settings as advanced generalists:

- From a focus on general knowledge to an emphasis on knowledge at the point of care with application and action in clinical situations
- From a movement from classroom and clinical instruction to integrating learning into practice
- From an emphasis on critical thinking to an approach of clinical reasoning and judgment that includes critical thinking
- From an emphasis on socialization and role taking to an emphasis on professional transformation through learning and reflective practice

They require the most comprehensive knowledge of evidence-based practice (EBP), patient care, quality and environmental care outcomes, team and group processes, systems thinking, and technology. A master's degree only helps them begin their journey into the next level of professional development through lifelong learning.

The second, more formal process of professional development for the CNL role is that of certification.

To use the CNL® title, Clinical Nurse Leaders must graduate from an accredited CNL® program and pass an examination. The Commission on Nurse Certification (CNC) is the credentialing body that oversees the certification of CNLs®.

For more information on certification, recertification, requirements, and exam dates visit:
http://www.aacn.nche.edu/cnc

For more information about certification, a CNL toolkit, conferences, and many other resources available, visit:
http://www.aacn.nche.edu/CNL/Index.htm

It is after receiving the master's degree and the CNL® certification that the continuing education journey really begins.

There are a variety of learning opportunities available to Clinical Nurse Leaders. Some may be familiar to the CNL; others, such as reflective practice or maintaining a professional portfolio, may be new. Everyone learns in a different way. It is important that each individual seeks out the approach and opportunities best suited to their individual learning style, which may include the following:

1. Continuing education programs that support their development in leadership, holding difficult conversations, change management, and information technology. These programs usually have continuing education hours/units associated with them and can be applied to meet the requirements of license renewal depending on the state the CNL practices in.

2. The Clinical Nurse Leader Association (CNLA) provides a national forum for CNLs to support, collaborate, and celebrate their unique and evolving role in all practice settings. The association highlights the benefits the CNL can bring to the organization, provides links to information on the CNL® certification, provides opportunities for CNLs to network (through their annual summit and quarterly newsletters), shares the successes and research from CNLs, and generally looks at advancing the role of the CNL in healthcare. Details of how to join can be found at http://www.cnlassociation.org. (Appendix 2)

3. Maintaining a professional portfolio. A professional portfolio is a collection of documents and certificates summarizing present and historical accomplishments, competencies, education, and experience (Harris & Roussel, 2010). It is an excellent tool for evaluating and translating knowledge, skills, and abilities into evidence of professional development and may include

- records of academic education and work;
- certificates of continuing education;
- resume and/or curriculum vitae (CV);
- copies of license, BLS/ACLS/PALS cards;
- copies of membership cards to professional organizations;
- examples of work - presentations, reports, writing samples;
- reference letters;
- reflective practice.

The portfolio needs to include evidence of professional development through the addition of new skills and by demonstrating growth in the competencies of their role. Some examples have been included in Figure 8.2.

It is important to note, there are no right or wrong pieces of evidence to place into a professional portfolio. The CNL just needs to make sure that HIPPA rules are adhered to so patients and specific staff cannot be identified in any of the contributions.

After the initial set-up time, a portfolio is easily updated. A useful tool for any nurse, it provides supporting evidence of the nurse's range of experience and learning outcomes to a manager or prospective employer.

4. Developing a habit of using reflective practice is a crucial skill for the CNL . Most nurses go through the reflective process to some degree naturally by identifying "that was a good day at work today" or, for example, following a successful resuscitation after a cardiac arrest, thinking that it "went well." Few take it to the next level to actually identify what they did that made something work well or in some cases did not.

Reflective practice is a structured process by which to unpick an experience or event in order to recognize that learning has occurred and future development needs identified.

The reflective process consists of a series of questions that enable the reflector to examine their performance, identify their subsequent learning needs (if any), and/or recognize whether they have effectively incorporated

Figure 8.2: Framework for Portfolio Content

Leadership and Change:
• Demonstrate the use of horizontal leadership in the care management process
• Introduce a change in the clinical areas, such as a new policy and reflecting on the approach used
• Include a reflective piece about a situation where a crucial conversation was used
• Demonstrate experience as a mentor for a new CNL
Knowledge Transfer:
• Copy of a conference presentation and the evaluations
• A grand round presentation
• Copy of an article published in the facility newsletter or in a nursing journal
• A reflective piece on the coaching and feedback for a direct caregiver
Outcomes Management:
• Carry out a clinical audit (include the tool and the report)
• A contribution to improve quality and care while reducing costs
• Provide evidence of improved clinical outcomes, such as decrease in falls, infections, pressure ulcers, and patient satisfaction scores
Interdisciplinary Relationships:
• Reflective piece on how a potential situation or conflict has been averted
• Nurse and interdisciplinary team satisfaction (360 degree assessment results)
• Evidence of being an effective care coordinator
Clinician at the Point of Care:
• Write and/or present a case study on the lateral integration of care for a patient with complex needs
• How and to what extent research and/or new evidence was incorporated into practice
Professional Development:
• Demonstrate the change/impact made after attending a continuing education program or conference and how this information was used to change/improve practice

new skills into their practice. It is important the reflective tool is quick and easy to use, such as the Framework for Reflection© (VHC, 2007), consisting of six simple questions applicable to any situation.

A Clinical Nurse Leader can reflect on any circumstance, positive or challenging; although, one area they are likely to use this approach, is with communication. For example,

They may have had a difficult conversation with a colleague about his/her noticeable lack of hand-washing between patents. This resulted in the nurse becoming defensive and the CNL becoming directive about the process. Ultimately, the CNL got the message through about the importance of hand-washing, but the relationship between the two was left strained and uncomfortable.

Using a reflective practice framework offers the CNL a way to objectively look at the experience, to reflect on the way it was handled, and identify what needs to be done to rebuild the relationship as well as avoid it happening again. The skill of being able to hold a difficult conversation with a colleague is one of high importance to any Clinical Nurse Leader's professional development.

Likewise, the reflective process can be used in groups and, when facilitated, may provide a particularly effective forum for CNLs to learn from each other.

It should be noted reflections are a personal thing and do not have to be shared in a portfolio if the individual is uncomfortable with that. What is important is the process and that it is incorporated as one of the tools in their lifelong learning journey.

5. Seeking a mentor is vital for new Clinical Nurse Leaders as they make the transition to this high profile role, one in which the organization is likely to have great expectations of them and which often causes increased stress. Different aspects of the role will present different challenges to each CNL. Therefore, they need to identify a mentor who

- has the professionalism, skills, patience, and standing within the organization they desire and can help them achieve their goals;
- is not their immediate manager.

A mentoring relationship is one of trust, confidentiality, and respect. While such qualities are possible in a relationship with their manager, the mentoring relationship needs to go beyond that which is normally associated between these two parties. The CNL/mentor relationship should exist at a level where CNLs may feel safe to honestly reflect on their experiences. Having their immediate manager as a mentor could cause them to close down to parts of the reflective process and lose the essence of what mentoring is about.

A good mentor/mentee relationship will include both parties agreeing to

- confidentiality;
- regular meetings;
- respecting each other's time;
- a relationship of trust and honesty;
- having something to offer;
- having specified goals;

- a regular review of the relationship.

The CNL's *preceptor* is best suited to be a fellow CNL, but, as more of them become experienced in their roles, their mentors might be members of another professional group. As long as their knowledge, skills, and abilities compliment the professional development needs of the CNL, this relationship can only enhance their development.

6. Attending organizational group meetings is perhaps the most informal of all tools for the CNL's professional development, as being in a new role can make them feel very isolated. While developing new ways of working, they are likely to be struggling with gaining understanding, acceptance, and partnership with their nursing colleagues and other professional groups. Initially there may not be enough CNLs to form a large cohort group. However, they should meet, as able, to discuss their daily challenges and solutions. One option for facilities with only a few CNLs, but who belong to a larger organizational network, is to facilitate conference calls.

7. Attending conferences is another great opportunity to network and share, take back some new ideas for their own facility and practice, and renew energy and enthusiasm for the role.

It is important that CNLs are able to negotiate their learning needs with their Nurse Manager in order to continue their professional development and build competencies that help them meet the needs of the organization, their patient populations, and themselves in their expanded role. This is a conversation they need to ensure happens far more frequently than the usual annual performance review.

The second part of the CNL's role in professional development is to participate in the growth and development of others.

As a thread running through the elements of the *Transforming Practice, Transforming Care™* model, their contributions to the professional development of others are continuous. These contributions provide a stimulating environment for building relationships, connecting to their team members, and remaining on the cutting edge of practice innovations and new knowledge. While many of their professional development activities are so much a part of their role they are not even obvious, such as their work with direct caregivers, some are more overt and include

- orienting and mentoring new CNLs;
- providing information to unit staff and team members, such as the latest research in practice changes to decrease nosocomial infections in post-surgical patients or a new policy;
- sharing their professional stories with others interested in becoming advanced generalists;
- presenting at grand rounds;
- providing feedback at unit meetings.

Whether seeking to meet their own professional development needs or those with whom they work, being Clinical Nurse Leaders means educating everyone within the facility of the scope of influence nursing can and does have in making a difference to patient outcomes.

POINT TO MAGNET

Clinical Nurse Leaders embrace lifelong learning, education (academic, continuing education, in-services, and career development), and competency-based clinical advancement as part of their structural empowerment in professional practice addressing organizational structure, personnel policies and programs, community and the healthcare organizations, the image of nursing, and professional development.

Structural empowerment in nursing practice is so critical the ANCC Magnet Recognition Program® identified this as one of five core components of their 2008 model. Through the changes and improvements they make at the point of care delivery and the intra and interdisciplinary relationships they develop, Clinical Nurse Leaders are ideally placed to empower the nursing staff they work with to achieve the best outcomes for their patients, reflecting the goals of the organization, profession, and community they serve, as they participate in the development of the structures and processes necessary for this to occur.

Clinical Nurse Leader:
Transforming Practice, Transforming Care

Chapter 9:
Successes, Challenges, & Opportunities for the CNL

As Clinical Nurse Leaders become more and more a part of the established communities of nursing practice, they will inevitably encounter a variety of opportunities and challenges along the road to achieving their goals. This final chapter looks at the successes that have already been demonstrated through the introduction of this role, the challenges that many CNLs have and will face during their journey, and the endless opportunities available to them in the future.

Much of the early work conducted in evaluating the impact of Clinical Nurse Leaders originated in the Veterans Administration Health Care System. They recognized the potential of this new role very early in its development and have seen some remarkable progress made in patient care outcomes in several different facilities (Ott et al, 2009), including the following:

- An increase in nursing hours per patient day (NHPPD) from 6.09 hours to 6.74 hours. It was felt this was due to the CNL facilitating problem solving, decision making, and improving patient flow.
- A reduction in sitter hours in one facility for patients with dementia, which resulted in a cost savings of $10,243, with sitter hours being reduced from 676 hours per month to just 24 hours with no loss of safety for the staff or the patient.
- An increase in staff compliance to providing discharge teaching to patients from 13% to

100% after the CNL developed new discharge materials. (It could logically be determined this would potentially have an impact on re-admissions.)

- A reduction in the incidence of ventilator assisted pneumonia from 21.7% to 8.7% following an intervention program developed by the unit CNL. The VA identified each incidence cost them $40,000.
- A 55% decrease in perioperative and gastrointestinal (GI) patient cancellations following intervention by the CNL.

This data clearly shows the potential financial benefits to the organization by employing CNLs as well as an improvement in patient outcomes. Also, it answers the question most facilities have about whether they can afford to hire them. When looking at their early successes, the question seems almost irrelevant.

Additionally, CNLs are making an impact beyond the VA Health Care System. The AHRQ Health Care Innovations Exchange (2010) recognized the introduction of the role in a Florida hospital led to better scores in the Centers for Medicare and Medicaid Services (CMS) Core Measures, reflecting a general increase from 90% to 100% over a period of two years. Furthermore, nurse turnover fell from 11.2% to 2.6% and increases reported in patient and physician satisfaction.

Following the introduction of Clinical Nurse Leaders into two large acute care units in a Florida Health Care System, Hartranft et al (2007) found in the areas that had "CNL rooms" there was a reduction to zero in falls with injury as well as a reduction in nosocomial infections and pressure ulcers. Not only did patient satisfaction increase, CNLs had an impact on their nursing colleagues, as well. Several nurses who had expressed a desire to leave the facility decided to stay following the introduction of the role in their area. Also, physicians were very supportive of Clinical Nurse Leaders whom they described as their "go to" person (p 263).

Knowing their patient cohort, liaising with other professional groups, relaying information back to nursing colleagues, and discussing appropriate interventions are crucial elements for the CNL role to function.

In fact, anecdotal evidence and ongoing research indicates that the introduction of Clinical Nurse Leaders has a direct effect in reducing the number of medical errors (the origins of the role), increasing nurses' satisfaction, reducing the number of patient complaints, and improving communication with their intra and interdisciplinary colleagues (an essential requirement in addressing the need for effective communication between disciplines to ensure patient safety).

***

One of the challenges in evaluating the impact of the CNL role is measuring what could be described as the "art" of nursing. While some interventions, such as the impact on discharge delays, infections, and deep vein thrombosis (DVT), are quantifiable and easily measured, such areas as the impact on patient and family satisfaction scores are not. It is important for a facility to identify how they are going to approach evaluation before they introduce the role. Many large healthcare organizations internally benchmark, or they may use tools, such as the percentile rating received from Press Ganey scores. Also, integrating questions in the annual staff survey may help determine the impact of the CNL. While it is the quantitative data that will provide the evidence of cost effectiveness to this role, it is important to retain the component that is *the essence of nursing.*

Even though we see evidence of the difference the Clinical Nurse Leader makes to patient outcomes, as well as non-clinical benefits, the role is not without its challenges and skeptics with many questions still being asked. (Appendix 3)

These are not totally unexpected and reflect the newness of this role. These challenges and questions include the following points:

- *A lack of clarity in the role.* There still remains much confusion and misunderstanding between the roles of the Clinical Nurse Specialist (CNS), Clinical Nurse Educator (CNE), and Clinical Nurse Leader (CNL). This is often made worse by the fact that some facilities have decided to replace a CNS or CNE with a CNL rather than recognize they are in fact different but complimentary. It is very confusing to staff, particularly those who have known the individual in the previous role and find it hard to recognize the difference. This replacement approach may well be due to a lack of funding. It should, however, be remembered the CNLs themselves could be having some challenges surrounding the clarity of their role and explaining it to their colleagues.

- ***The organization not clearly understanding why they want a CNL.*** To send/support an individual nurse to complete a master's program that enables them to undertake the exam to become a certified CNL® without having a clear business case that underpins the need for the role and its expected benefits to patient care, is to set the role and the individual up to fail. It is imperative the nurse executive understands the rationale for the introduction of a CNL and is active in marketing it to other nurse leaders.

- ***The Clinical Nurse Leader (CNL) not being empowered to do the job.*** While being uniquely positioned to meet the organizational and unit goals relating to safe, high quality patient care, the CNL exists within a system of a traditional vertical hierarchy that frequently leads to delays in decision making. Their role as a horizontal leader may be initially misunderstood and could result in a resistance to its integration. It is essential Nurse Managers, in particular, are fully briefed on the way the CNL needs to function within their team, the level of authority and autonomy required for their effectiveness, and the support needed as the CNL markets the new role to intra and interdisciplinary colleagues.

- ***A lack of a support network for the CNL in order to avoid silo working.*** Strong relationships are crucial for the CNL to function effectively, and they need to have a strong communication network that enables them to have some input into the planning of clinical outcomes at the meso and macro systems level. Also, they require opportunities to meet with one another to share their successes and discuss the best ways to accomplish the organizational and patient care goals.

- *A lack of flexibility in the role.* The CNL is a new role, and while the principles of practice are the same there will need to be some flexibility in how it is established in different clinical settings, especially where the assigned caseload and expected outcomes may be different. This is definitely a case of *"one size does not fit all."*

- *The evaluation criteria are not established before the CNL starts to work in this role.* Identifying some key measures by which the success of the role will be established need to be stated in the business case prior to implementation. Without a clear target, it is difficult to provide direction to the role and establish relationships. Also, it is a very helpful tool for CNLs to have when explaining to their peers and other professional groups why their role was introduced. There needs to be some flexibility in the setting of the criteria, but a solid starting point will help provide some purpose to the role as the CNL settles into the organizational structure.

- *Lack of opportunity for networking outside the organization.* New CNLs need to be given the opportunity to attend the annual CNLA summit and other events that provide them with an opportunity to share their experiences and gain new information they can bring back to the facility. Networking can be combined with an aspect of the CNL's own professional development -- their presentation skills. They may be able to submit an abstract for a conference presentation and, if accepted, provide the facility with a means of raising their profile, all the while saving money as most speakers get travel, hotel, and complimentary registration paid for by conference organizers.

***

With the successes identified and the challenges discussed, it seems appropriate to end this book with a look at the opportunities available now and in the future for the role of the Clinical Nurse Leader.

There can be little doubt with the passing of The Patient Protection and Affordable Care Act in March 2010 millions of Americans are going to experience increased access to healthcare, particularly in the areas of primary care and prevention. This act provides an ideal opportunity for the CNL to contribute to the achievement of high quality care in all environments and influence outcomes at every level of service for their patient populations.

The Veterans Health Administration's Office of Nursing Services (ONS) set a national strategic goal for Clinical Nurse Leaders to be implemented at every point of care within its healthcare system by 2016.

Their nursing leaders noted the positive relationship between the educational preparation of the CNL, direct caregivers, and the quality of care outcomes, and became a committed partner in developing and advancing the Clinical Nurse Leader (CNL) role. This commitment was made as part of their national strategic plan for recognizing this, along with the need for new and different nursing roles to provide greater accountability and enhanced care management and coordination at the point of care.

The CNL role provides a wonderful career option for experienced nurses who wish to stay at the point of care rather than follow the more traditional paths of management or formal education.

Many organizations have implemented the role into their nursing services and included them in their career ladders. They recognize and respect the graduate level education, broad clinical skills, and expertise of these clinicians at the point at which care is delivered and have provided a role to which nurses may aspire.

The CNL® is a unique credential that recognizes the excellence of the direct caregiver in

- analyzing the patient care climates and cultures of healthcare organizations;
- influencing change through horizontal and transformational leadership;
- implementing evidenced-based practice and practice-based evidence to support and guide the nursing care of complex patient cohorts.

"Although the jury is still out on the long-term success of the CNL role on a national level, [their] experience with the role has led to a belief that this innovative nursing role holds much promise to promote a healthier work environment at the unit level. The CNLs have the ability to transform the care environment in a

manner that elevates professional nursing practice, ensures quality outcomes, complies with core measures, and creates an environment in which nurses feel supported and empowered" (Sherman et al, 2009, p 270).

In fact, the CNL may be the role that pulls together the fragmented care that has been for so long the cause of much miscommunication and medical errors, ensuring patients, wherever they are in the healthcare continuum, receive safe, evidence-based, quality care.

POINT TO MAGNET

Many diverse and complex factors challenge clinicians today in every practice setting and environment of care. Magnet designation has become an icon for organizations actively involved in meeting those challenges and embracing the future leaders in the delivery of healthcare worldwide. Clinical Nurse Leaders who have a strong understanding of and who work by the core Magnet principles, who are innovative, entrepreneurial (Guo, 2009) and passionate about what they do are ideal leaders to embrace the changes required of healthcare reform wherever their clients are seen.

Appendix 1: CNL Standards of Conduct

The *CNL Standards of Conduct* refers to a set of principles, core values, and behaviors identified for Clinical Nurse Leaders[SM] (CNL®) certified or recertified by the Commission on Nurse Certification (CNC, 2010), an autonomous arm of the American Association of Colleges of Nursing (AACN).

The five standards of

- altruism,
- accountability,
- human dignity,
- integrity, and
- social justice

underpin the CNL's practice in providing safe, humanistic health care while maintaining competencies in these areas through continuing education.

While their interpretation and application have many facets, their core essence is exemplified below:

1. *I would rather be kept alive in the efficient, if cold, **altruism** of a large hospital, than expire in a gush of warm sympathy in a small one.*

   - Aneurin Bevan

Clinical Nurse Leaders align themselves with their patients/patient populations and healthcare team members by building strong therapeutic and professional relationships motivated by the compassion and cooperation needed to achieve safe, effective care outcomes. Through such activities as advocacy, risk assessment and management, and conflict resolution, they promote the well being of others in healing environments. As nurses, they also instill warmth and caring into their altruism.

2. *There is a positive trend that can continue indefinitely, but the price is that we have to pay attention and reward **accountability**. The new mantra for health care purchasers needs to be, 'show us your data.' Why trust your family's health to an organization that operates behind closed doors?*

    - Margaret E. O'Kane

Clinical Nurse Leaders accept accountability for their assigned patient populations and demonstrate horizontal leadership through shared decision making, safe and ethical care practices at point of care delivery, and outcomes management with the power to act on their clinical judgments. They engage in and implement evidence-based practice (EBP), collect and analyze patient data, and monitor changes related to quality improvement activities across multiple systems within the infrastructure of their organization and their unit. They evaluate and respond to health care modifications and interventions to improve outcomes. They are responsible for their own practice and are accountable to their team members, patients, and communities for their decisions, actions, and competencies.

3. *What should move us to action is **human dignity**: the inalienable dignity of the oppressed, but also the dignity of each of us. We lose dignity if we tolerate the intolerable.*

    - Unknown

Clinical Nurse Leaders are nurses who demonstrate profound respect for their team members and patients and advocate for them. They care for the most vulnerable ones among us, *i.e.*, the sick, lost, broken, and damaged ones, those without hope or who are shrouded in pain, sorrow, or dementia. They uncover the inherent value within each person they serve by being culturally aware, confidential of sensitive and/or private information, and always remembering the worth and dignity of every human soul they encounter at the point of care delivery and among those who serve with them.

4. *Integrity is doing the right thing, even if nobody is watching.*

- Unknown

Clinical Nurse Leaders are nurses who embrace their professional code of ethics and act accordingly, *i.e.*, with honesty and in the provision of care based on the principles and application of an ethical framework that is accepted within the profession, through their documentation, and in the supervision of those they lead.

5. *Until the great mass of the people shall be filled with the sense of responsibility for each other's welfare, social justice can never be attained.*

- Helen Keller

Clinical Nurse Leaders work closely with Social Services, *e.g.*, to provide resources for patients transitioning from the clinical unit to home. They use their knowledge of healthcare organizations, community services, and care opportunities to help their patients receive ongoing access to whatever resources they need when discharged to their homes and families. When a patient is homeless, the interdisciplinary team explores options through all available venues, *i.e.*, homeless shelters, skilled nursing homes, etc., while holding to moral, legal, and compassionate principles when considering treatment interventions. They participate in health care reform to advance nursing and explore better care options to patients and their families regardless of sociopolitical or economic standing.

Appendix 2: Clinical Nurse Leader Association (CNLA)

Clinical Nurse Leader Association

The Clinical Nurse Leader Association (CNLA) was formed through a collaborative effort with the initial Clinical Nurse Leader (CNL) graduates and key stake holders in 2008 . The official presentation of the CNLA occurred at the 2009 American Association of Colleges of Nursing (AACN) CNL summit in New Orleans. We have enjoyed a steady growth rate along with the ever increasing numbers of CNLs and also boast members from coast to coast and from varying organizations including hospitals, universities and community settings. Our mission is to provide a forum for members in all practice settings to collaborate, collect data, publish results, network, maintain a professional presence and stay abreast of issues affecting their practice. Our vision is to improve patient outcomes through a focus on safety and quality outcomes and the implementation of evidence based practice at the point of care. Microsystem analysis, designing patient focused plans of care, meeting or exceeding reportable standards of practice and reducing non-refundable hospital acquired events are examples of how a CNL® can add value to cost containment efforts and improved patient outcomes. Providing continuing education credits for our members, participation in conferences, web based forums and quarterly newsletters are examples of how we meet the needs of our members. Membership categories for the CNLA include practicing

Clinical Nurse Leader:
Transforming Practice, Transforming Care

CNLs, CNL students, educators and practice partners. For further information or to obtain membership visit our web site at www.cnlassociation.org.

Mary Stachowiak MSN, RN, CNL
President CNLA

Appendix 3: Q & A from the Field

I am a Wound Ostomy Continence Nurse (WOCN) and have been asked by my Manager to attend the CNL master's program. Can a WOCN be a CNL?

The WOCN is the latest role to be recognized as a specialty by the American Nurses Association (ANA) and has a complimentary but different role to the Clinical Nurse Leader. The differences between the Clinical Nurse Specialist (CNS) and the Clinical Nurse Leader (CNL) are highlighted on page 4 in this book, but in general the CNS focuses on one specific type of population (in your case, patients that have wounds or ostomies), whereas the CNL is an *advanced generalist* and may have a variety of different types of patients in their care such as those seen in a med/surg unit. Secondly, the CNL functions in a particular unit or geographical area with a *defined* cohort of patients unlike a CNS who generally works on a referral basis as I am sure you are likely to do. Many of the modules in the master's program will be of benefit to you, but some will not and you may want to consider a program that provides areas such as leadership and change in order to strengthen your skills as a CNS rather than blur the boundaries between the two roles.

Whenever there is a shortage of staff on the unit my Nurse Manager makes me take a patient caseload, and I am unable to perform my CNL duties. How can I convince her that this is not what I do?

This is a common problem for many new CNLs and is often the result of a lack of understanding by the Nurse Manager and the organization of the role. Take some time to explain to them and your colleagues what the

CNL is about, what you can bring to the healthcare team, and how you can help the Nurse Manager meet the unit and organizational goals. Provide some literature for them to read on the role and the difference CNLs have already made. If there is more than one CNL in your facility, it may also be helpful to obtain some time at the next Nurse Managers meeting to present more information on the CNL and seek to enlist the help of the Chief Nursing Officer or VP Patient Care Services. Use as many opportunities as you can to let colleagues know about your role and give them time to assimilate the information. Be open to questions, be proactive, and try to be patient. Change is a process that cannot be rushed.

I have completed the CNL master's program and have just received my certification, but I am scared that I have no practical leadership experience. How can I improve this?

Start by finding a leader to mentor you. Build a relationship of mutual trust and respect then ask your mentor about leadership training and gaining practical experience. Study successful leaders in the organization—who is transformational (leads by influence), who is transactional (a micromanager)—and compare their styles. Discuss your observations and reflections with your mentor. The best leadership experience comes from doing it. It just takes time and a good mentor.

Why do people keep insisting that my CNL master's degree is not an advanced practice degree?

The term *advanced* in advanced generalist confuses some who argue that the CNL is not an advanced nurse practitioner. And they are right. Help them correct their perception of the role by teaching them the proper terminology, what you do, why being certified as a CNL requires a master's degree (an advanced degree), and how the advanced degree enhances your value and ability to contribute to the organization.

I received my RN license last year and want to undertake the CNL master's program. Is it too soon for me to do this?

While many of the CNL master's programs do not require a minimum amount of clinical or leadership experience, we believe that becoming an advanced generalist with the full scope of responsibility and accountability that comes with an assigned patient population requires at least 3-5 years of clinical experience to be competent and confident enough to take on this role. Knowledge can always be achieved quickly. Wisdom and the ability to make good clinical judgments demands more.

Everyone talks about the CNL role being a point of care practitioner and tells me I have to spend 100% of my time with direct care providers. Is this correct?

No. The CNL is also involved in risk management, quality systems, data collection and analysis, and outcomes management that all require interdisciplinary communications, resource allocations, and networking. The CNL is responsible—accountable—for a patient population (maybe 20-30 patients), not a patient assignment (usually 2-6 patients). Direct care providers are important members of the team but do not require attention 100% of the time.

I have been asked by my nurse manager to be a preceptor to one of the new nurses on our unit. I did not want to say no but do not think that I should be doing this.

The CNL role is not about taking away responsibility from other nurses *who are* preceptors. They generally only formally precept and/or mentor other CNLs, or those staff with similar scopes of practice, opportunities, and challenges. However, that does not mean that they do not work with the nurse who is being preceptored. CNLs work with all the direct caregivers who are involved with their defined cohort of patients/clients at the point of care so it is inevitable that they will be involved with educating the preceptee, and likely that they will provide feedback to the preceptor on their progress.

Regarding staffing effectiveness, do we need a CNL on every shift? What hours does a CNL work?

The determination of what hours the CNL works is ultimately the decision of the unit they are employed within and organizational preference. If there is only one CNL on the unit then it is recommended that they work during the day to enable them to coordinate care with other health care professionals, provide health education, promotion, and discharge advice to patients and their families, and spend time with the direct caregivers. It is also suggested that the CNL does not work the first or second shift, but has their own hours that cross the shifts not only to maximize their exposure to the staff, but also to define the role as different to the regular floor nurse. However, there is a definite need for staff who work on the night shift to understand the role and have the same level of support from the CNL as those who work days, so some flexibility is definitely recommended, particularly in the early stages.

I work in a long term care facility and would really like to become a CNL. How can I convince the Director of Nursing and the Administrator that it is worth them supporting the development of this role?

Present your case in an objective manner that includes all the benefits that the role will bring to them, the residents, and their families. Include evidence of how CNLs have already made an impact on areas such as infections, staff retention, patient and staff satisfaction, and in particular seek out evidence of their impact in the areas that Medicare have defined as preventable conditions such as pressure ulcers and falls. Speak to the Risk Manager to obtain the data for the facility that relates to these areas, ensure that you include areas that you could impact, such as the documentation for Minimum Data Set, Version 3.0 (MDS 3.0), Accreditation Commission for Healthcare (ACHA), or Joint Commission, gather information on the role, and even write a draft job description. Present all your data in a formal business case clearly demonstrating how they can realize a return on their investment by supporting your development in this role.

It has been really difficult to get the interdisciplinary team to understand why I am involved more in some patients than others when they said they managed perfectly well without me before. I really don't know what to say.

It is very difficult to suddenly become part of an established clinical team and it will take time for your interdisciplinary team members to accept the CNL role. Change causes resistance and resistance results in behavioral changes. The most important thing to do at this point is to be sure that you fully understand their concerns and answer any questions. The best way to do this is to 'walk in their shoes for a day', one by one. This not only provides you with an opportunity to get to know what they do from their perspective, but also opens up an opportunity for you to explain in more detail your role and answer any questions in the safety of a one on one situation. An understanding of change management, learning the dynamics of the team, being available to answer any questions on the role, not taking resistance personally, putting yourself in their situation, and being patient are the keys to obtaining their understanding of your role and including you in their team.

References

American Association of Colleges of Nursing (AACN). (2007). *White Paper on the Education and Role of the Clinical Nurse Leader^SM*. Retrieved April 17, 2010 from AACN: Official Web site: http://www.aacn.nche.edu/publications/whitepapers/clinicalnurseleader.htm.

Agency for Healthcare Research and Quality (AHRQ) Health Care Innovations Exchange. (2010). Implementing Clinical Nurse Leader Role Improves Core Measures Performance, Patient and Physician Satisfaction and Reduces Nurse Turnover; American Association of Colleges of Nursing; Florida Atlantic University; St. Lucie Medical Center. In: AHRQ Health Care Innovations Exchange [Web site]. Rockville (MD): [cited May 2010]. Available: http://www.innovations.ahrq.gov/content.aspx?id=2566.

American Nursing Credentialing Center (ANCC). (2008). *The Magnet Model Components and Sources of Evidence: Magnet Recognition Program®*. Silver Spring, MD: ANCC.

Benner, P. (1984). *From Novice to Expert: Excellence and Power in Clinical Nursing Practice*. Menlo- Park, CA: Addison-Wesley.

Benner, P., Sutphen, M., Leonard, V., & Day, L. (2010). *Educating Nurses: A Call for Radical Transformation*. San Francisco, CA: Jossey-Bass/Carnegie Foundation for the Advancement of Teaching.

Black, J. S., & Gregersen, H. B. (2008). *It Starts with One: Changing Individuals Changes Organizations*. Upper Saddle River, NJ: Wharton School Publishing.

Blanchard, K., & Hodges, P. (2003). *The Servant Leader: Transforming Your Heart, Head, Hands & Habits*. Nashville, TN: Thomas Nelson Incorporated.

Case Management Society of America (CMSA). (2002). *Standards of Practice for Case Management.* Little Rock, AK: CMSA.

Commission on Nurse Certification. (2010). Clinical Nurse Leader[SM] (CNL®) Standards of Conduct. Retrieved April 17, 2010 from AACN: Official Web site: http://www.aacn.nche.edu/cnc/pdf/SOC.pdf.

Cooperrider, D., & Whitney, D. (2005). *Appreciative Inquiry: A Positive Revolution in Change.* San Francisco, CA: Berrett-Koehler Publishers.

Edouard-Trevathan, E. (April 2010). The Clinical Nurse Leader: A Catalyst in Community Healthcare Transformation. *Nurse Leader, 8*(2), 25-28.

Felgen, J. (2007). *I₂E₂: Leading Lasting Change.* Minneapolis, MN: Creative Health Care Management, Inc.

Guo, K. (2009). Core Competencies of the Entrepreneurial Leader in Health Care Organizations. *The Health Care Manager, 28*(1), 19-29.

Habel M. & Yoder L. (2007) Coaching Makes Nurses' Careers Grow. CE432. Retrieved May 2010 from: http://ce.nurse.com/ce432/CoursePage.

Hartranft, S., Garcia, T., & Adams, N. (2007). Realizing the Anticipated Effects of the Clinical Nurse Leader. *The Journal of Nursing Administration.* 37(6), 261-263.

Harris, J.L., & Roussel, L. (Eds.). (2010). *Initiating and Sustaining the Clinical Nurse Leader Role: A Practical Guide.* Sudbury, MA: Jones & Bartlett.

Hendrich A., Fay J., & Sorrels A. (2004). Effects of Acuity-Adaptable Rooms on Flow of Patients and Delivery of Care. *American Journal of Critical Care,13,35-45.*

Hersey, P., & Blanchard, D. (1988). *Management of Organizational Behavior: Utilizing Human Resources.* (5th ed.). Englewood Cliffs, New Jersey: Prentice-Hall.

Institute of Medicine. (1999). *To Err is Human: Building a Safer Health System.* Washington, DC: National Academy Press.

Institute of Medicine. (2003). *Health Professions Education: A Bridge to Quality.* Retrieved June 2010 from: http://www.acme-assn.org/valuable_resources/IOM-ABridgetoQuality.pdf.

Jessop R. (2007). Interdisciplinary versus multi-disciplinary teams: do we understand the difference? *Australian Health Review.* August 12, 2010 accessed 07/31/10 at www.findarticles.com/p/articles/mi_6800/is_3_31/ai_n28446050

Kovner, C., Brewer, C., Yingrengreung, S., & Fairchild S. (2010). New Nurses' Views of Quality Improvement Education. *Joint Commission Journal on Quality and Patient Safety, 36(1), 29-5AP (-23).*

Lewin, K. (1951). *Field Theory in Social Science: Selected Theoretical Papers.* New York, NY: Harper & Row.

Maxfield, D., Grenny, J., McMillan, R., Patterson, K., & Switzler, A. (2005). Silence Kills - The Seven Crucial Conversations® in Healthcare. (Vitalsmarts™). Retrieved May 27, 2010, from: http://www.silencekills.com/UPDL/SilenceKillsExecSummary.pdf.

Ott, K., Haddock, S., Fox, S., Shinn, J., Walters, S., Hardin, J., Durrand, K., & Harris, J. (2009). The Clinical Nurse Leader[SM]: Impact on Practice Outcomes in the Veterans Health Administration. *Nurse Economics, 27(6), 363-370.*

Patterson, K., Grenny, J., McMillan, R., & Switzler, A. (2002). *Crucial Conversations: Tools for Talking When Stakes are High.* New York, NY: McGraw-Hill.

Sherman, R. O., Edwards, B., Giovengo, K., & Hilton, N. (2009). The Role of the Clinical Nurse Leader in

Promoting a Healthy Work Environment at the Unit Level. *Critical Care Nursing Quarterly, 32(4), 264-271.*

Strenger, Rob. (2007). The Medical Home Model of Primary Care: Implications for the Healthy Oregon Act. Retrieved July 2010 from: http://www.oregon.gov/OHPPR/docs/The_Medical_H ome_Model_Final.pdf?ga=t.

Studer, Q. (2004). *The Power of Hourly Rounding: Call Light Study Proves Proactive Approach Boosts Patient Satisfaction and Nurse Morale.* Retrieved June 2010 from: http://www.obgyn.net/menopause/menopause.asp? page=/nursing/news/nurse_morale.

Terra, S. (2007). An Evidence-Based Approach to Case Management Model Selection for an Acute Care Facility: Is There Really a Preferred Model? *Professional Case Management, 12(3), 147-157.*

Visioning HealthCare (VHC). (2007). *Framework for Reflection©.* Sarasota, FL: Visioning Healthcare.

Glossary

Direct caregiver: A licensed nurse and/or certified care assistant who works in the same microsystem as the Clinical Nurse Leader and is responsible for the delivery of clinical care.

Environmental scanning: The systematic research of information via internet, journal, associations, and colleagues both internal and external to the organization in order to inform planning and decision making.

Functional Silos: Departments that work in isolation of others within the same organization and develop physical and communication barriers with other departments and units.

Horizontal Leadership: An approach where the leader's influence is earned through knowledge, education and respect, and which engages members of the intra and interdisciplinary teams in creating an environment of learning, accountability, synergy, and problem-solving.

Interdisciplinary: A group of professionals who work collaboratively to determine and deliver a shared goal that is patient, rather than professionally, focused.

Interprofessional: A minimum of two or more professional groups working together to achieve a shared purpose/goal.

Intradisciplinary: A group of people from one's own discipline.

Lateral Integration: A process of coordinating, facilitating and overseeing the clinical care provided by the intra and interdisciplinary teams in order to reduce the fragmentation of the care received by the patient.

Multi-disciplinary: A group of health professionals who meet to discuss the care, treatment, and progress of their patients, but who individually assess them and determine discipline specific goals.

Professional Silos: Professional groups that work independently rather than collaboratively and whom develop invisible barriers toward working with others.

Servant leadership: A style or philosophy wherein the leader works, through a process of collaboration, trust, and honesty in serving the staff they lead in order for them to grow and flourish.

Transformational Leadership: An approach where the leader has a vision of where they need to go, and through a process of trust, integrity and influence leads their followers in getting there.

Vertical Leadership: A position of leadership where the power and the authority of the leader is received purely from their position within the vertical hierarchy of the organization.

VISIONING HEALTHCARE

Order Form

Mail completed form to:
Visioning HealthCare Inc.
6731 Professional Parkway W, Suite 105
Sarasota, FL 34240
Order by phone: 1-877-823-4310
Order online: www.visioninghealthcare.com

Books:

Product	Price	Quantity	Total
Clinical Nurse Leader: *Transforming Practice, Transforming Care*	$29.95		
Shipping & Handling:			$ 6.95
Additional Shipping Charges - for multiple books add $1.00 per book			
Add sales tax if in Florida only:			
Total Charges:			

Tools:

Product	Price	Quantity	Total
Clinical Nurse Leader: *Transforming Practice, Transforming Care* *A model for the clinician at the point of care.* Pocket-Sized Tool - 4 x 6 in.			
Framework for Reflection© Pocket-Sized Tool - 4 x 6 in.			
Quantity Per Tool Price 1-20 $1.55 each 21-50 $1.35 each 51-100 $1.15 each 101-500 $1.05 each 501-1000 $0.95 each			
Shipping & Handling *(up to 50 tools)*:			$ 2.95
Additional Shipping Charges - per extra 25 tools, add $1.00			
Add sales tax if in Florida only:			
Total Charges:			

Fill in contact and payment information on the back of this form.

Please check our website for associated handbooks and workshops.
www.visioninghealthcare.com

VISIONING HEALTHCARE

Order Form

Mail completed form to:
Visioning HealthCare Inc.
6731 Professional Parkway W, Suite 105
Sarasota, FL 34240
Order by phone: 1-877-823-4310
Order online: www.visioninghealthcare.com

Contact Information:

Name *(Please print legibly)*

Organization (if applicable)

Street Address

City, State ZIP

Email Address (for shipping confirmation and updates)

Phone Number

Payment Information:

Payment Method: MasterCard/Visa/Discover/Check   Make checks payable to Visioning HealthCare Inc.

/ /

Card Number   Exp. Date   CID #

Name on Card

Authorizing Signature

Please check our website for associated handbooks and workshops.
www.visioninghealthcare.com.